MADISON GHOSTS AND LEGENDS

MADISON GHOSTS AND LEGENDS

ANNA LARDINOIS

Published by Haunted America
A Division of The History Press
Charleston, SC
www.historypress.com

Front cover: Wisconsin state capitol. *Anna Lardinois.*

First published 2022

Manufactured in the United States

ISBN 9781467150194

Library of Congress Control Number: 2022937897

To the spook-tacular Corey Lardinois
and every ghost's favorite editor, John Rodrigue.

CONTENTS

CONTENTS

ACKNOWLEDGEMENTS

N o person accomplishes anything alone, and it is in that spirit I'd like to thank the following people and groups, without whom I could not have started on my spook-tacular journey.

I offer a tip of the hat to Mike Huberty, owner of American Ghost Walks and creator of the Haunted Madison tour, for keeping folklore and paranormal enthusiasm alive in Dane County and beyond.

With gratitude, I acknowledge the Wisconsin Historical Society, whose tireless chronicling of Badger State happenings has created a treasure trove of information that is dear to all who love to explore the past.

With appreciation, I acknowledge my acquisitions editor, John Rodrigue, whose incredible patience makes him a delight to work with.

ON A PERSONAL NOTE, I would like to acknowledge the special support and patronage of the following very dear people: the Bonesteels, the Merbeths, the Peck Row Posse and my cheerleaders Caroline, Jackie, Jen, Jill and Wendy.

Finally, an enormous thank you to Corey Lardinois, whose support, encouragement and unfailing patience have made all things possible.

PREFACE

Celebrated Wisconsin folklorist Robert E. Gard once claimed that Wisconsin has more ghosts per square mile than any other state. While his assertion is impossible to prove, there does seem to be something about Wisconsin that compels restless spirits to remain among the living. There is no part of the state that does not have its own haunted buildings, celebrated specters and eerie local legends. Madison, Wisconsin's capital city, is no exception. The City of Four Lakes is rife with supernatural tales waiting to be discovered by the curious.

It would be impossible to create a book of otherworldly tales without the efforts of many talented people. No collection of Wisconsin folklore and ghostly tales would be complete without the acknowledgement of Dr. Charles E. Brown (1872–1946). The Milwaukee-born Brown devoted most of his professional life to "the collection, study, and preservation of Wisconsin folklore history, archeology and Indian lore," according to his professional papers, which are housed in the Wisconsin Historical Society. He headed the Wisconsin State Historical Society for thirty-six years as its chief curator. A faculty member at the University of Wisconsin from 1914 to 1944, he also led the Wisconsin Folklore Society for sixteen years, in addition to holding leadership roles in an impressive number of academic societies. As the head of the Wisconsin division of the Federal Writers' Project, which ran from 1935 to 1942, Brown hired scores of writers and researchers to capture and record strange local tales that passed from one generation to another orally. The Works Progress Administration (WPA) preserved hundreds of

Wisconsin stories, a number of which are featured in this book. Without Brown's efforts, many of these tales would have likely been lost.

Whereas Brown is revered for his collection of traditional tales, the modern masters keeping the otherworldly tales of the past alive should also be acknowledged. Beth Scott and Michael Norman's *Haunted Wisconsin* collection elevated the genre of ghost stories while preserving more contemporary tales. The pair, and their seminal book, are an inspiration for most midwestern storytellers to this day. Another influential chronicler of the unusual is Linda Godfrey. She is credited with introducing the country to the famed Beast of Bray Road and has worked tirelessly to record Wisconsin oddities. Without Godfrey's books, much of Wisconsin's most colorful history would go unknown by all but a lucky few. These writers, and countless others, ensure we remain connected to the past and our history.

Nearly every time I tell my strange and spooky tales, I am asked, "How do you find your stories?" I find my stories in countless ways. Some of the stories are discovered in books just like this one, written by well-known Wisconsin writers working in this genre. I also spend a great deal of time inside local historical societies' reading rooms, looking through dusty volumes for hints of legends to explore. Newspaper archives—in the form of microfilm, microfiche and digitally preserved newspapers that can be accessed online— are my key source of material. Sometimes, if I am very lucky, I will stumble upon a tale whispered to me in an out-of-the-way location. When that happens, the story usually comes with enough information that I can begin to track down details of these lesser-known tales.

While we have yet to identify a way to definitively prove the existence of ghosts, every effort has been made to ensure the historical accuracy of the stories presented in the book. When names, dates or other factual evidence are presented, the information obtained is the result of academic research. All sources used for this collection of tales can be found in the bibliography of this book.

From childhood, I have always loved stories. I was both attracted and repelled by ghostly tales. They thrilled me but never failed to give me nightmares. As a kid, for me, ghost stories were all about the bloody specter in the mirror or the terrible hook embedded in the car door. As I got older, I grew to appreciate scary stories beyond the visceral reaction they cause. I discovered that ghost stories are a wonderful way to access the history of a city and to make the past come alive. It is a true love of storytelling that brings me to collect stories of the supernatural. I have found long Wisconsin winters are perfect for snuggling up next to the fire and reading eerie tales of otherworldly events while the wind howls through barren tree branches. I have spent many nights curled up under blankets while poring over tomes dedicated to the restless spirits of those who are no longer living but have yet to cross to the other side.

Because of the stories I've chosen to tell, some wonder whether I believe in ghosts. For me, the answer is a bit more complicated than a simple yes. I believe in the existence of ghosts, and I think the world is full of mysteries that humans do not understand. Ghostly tales captivate me, but ghost hunting does not. When I explore a story, the thing that most intrigues me are the people behind the haunting. When I get a report of supernatural activity, but I can't find out who the spirit is or, more importantly, why it remains in the earthly realm, it is very unlikely that I will retell the story, regardless of how much proof of paranormal activity is presented. For me, the answer to the questions "who" and "why" are the most essential parts of the story.

For example, seeing a glass move by an unseen hand or hearing a door slam in an empty home is interesting, but knowing the source of the activity is a woman who took her final, painful breath in the building before she died is the essence of a truly spinetingling tale.

My interest in ghosts, stories and history has made me an avid fan of ghost tours. These tours quickly became my favorite way to explore new cities, and I still take a tour in each city I visit. My love of participating in ghost tours led me to create Gothic Milwaukee, my own haunted, historical walking tour, in Milwaukee in 2012. The small tour was recognized by USA Today in 2016 as one of the "10 Must-See Halloween Events in Wisconsin"; in 2017, AAA Living identified the tour in its listing of three of the best tours in the state; and in 2019, the tour earned a GEMmy from the Midwest Travel Journalist Association. Gothic Milwaukee has been featured in the *LA Times* and the *Chicago Tribune* and has won a number of local awards. I am very proud of the tour and excited to be able to provide ghost story enthusiasts spooky stories from my beloved city.

CHAPTER 1

MADISON'S MOST CREEPY CAMPUS

The home of Bucky Badger may be one of the most haunted spots in Wisconsin's capital city. The University of Wisconsin was enacted by Nelson Dewey, the state's first governor, in 1848, the year Wisconsin achieved statehood. The fifty-acre plot of land chosen for the campus was beautifully situated on the shores of Lake Mendota. Unfortunately, when construction began on the first building, then known as University Hall, the site was rumored to have a dark reputation among the area's Native settlers

University of Wisconsin campus circa 1907. *Public domain.*

and had originally been used as a burial ground for the early European settlers. From the time the first building was completed in 1859 until today, strange tales of spooky happenings have been reported on the campus of the celebrated school.

BASCOM'S BONES

Bascom Hall: 500 Lincoln Drive

Most people know Bascom Hall was built on the site of a former graveyard. The land was a cemetery for white settlers from 1837 until 1846, and before that, it was used by Natives as a burial ground. Madisonians later decided the property could be put to better use, so the graves were excavated and the bodies reinterred elsewhere. Well, at least most of the bodies were removed from the land. Not all of them made it to their new resting place.

That eerie fact was revealed in 1918, when preparations were being made to erect the now well-known statue of Abraham Lincoln. Construction workers made an unexpected discovery while digging a base for the statue. The men uncovered two sets of human leg bones.

It was soon discovered that the four legs they unearthed were not those of contemporary murder victims. By examining the debris that surrounded the bones, which included a few iron nails and a shirt button, it was determined the bodies were those of early settlers, which were mistakenly left behind when the cemetery was moved. The leg bones were removed, and construction work in the area continued. But there were still surprises in store for the men working on this project.

In 1922, the bodies that had once been connected to the leg bones found in 1918 were discovered. The skeletons were found intact, with the exception of their missing legs. The bones were soon identified as the remains of William Nelson and Samuel Warren. Nelson had the distinction of being the first white settler to die in Madison. He died of typhoid and was laid to rest in 1837. Samuel Warren, who lived in the same rooming house as Nelson, died as result of a lightning strike in 1838. After the bodies were disinterred, it was decided that they would remain at rest on the land where they had spent nearly a century.

You can find these graves southwest of the landmark Lincoln statue. Two small brass plates, one marked "W.N. 1837" and the other "S.W. 1838," identify the burial site of two of Madison's earliest white settlers.

"U of Wisconsin, Madison" by Restless Journeyman. *Licensed under CC BY-NC-ND 2.0.*

Perhaps it is the spirits of the two men who remain buried on the land that are the source of the reported paranormal activity in and around Bascom Hall. But it also might be the restless spirits of those whose corpses were moved from the land. Or possibly even those whose bodies remain buried on Bascom Hill but undiscovered. We will likely never know the source of the paranormal activity on the land. But it is clear something continues to linger in the area, due to the many reports of supernatural activity in the area.

Generations of students have described hearing strange whispers while walking inside the empty hall. The unintelligible murmurs, whose source is unknown, have sent chills down many spines over the years. Sightings of specters abound, from a ghostly form spotted walking on the front stairs of Bascom Hall to full-body apparitions seen near the site of Nelson and Warren's graves. Some have even claimed to capture traces of these otherworldly beings in photos taken around the Lincoln statue.

Spooky Stacks

Memorial Library: 728 State Street

Memorial Library is home to the largest single collection of research material in Wisconsin, and if you believe the legends, the spirit of a celebrated former professor is there as well.

For years, it has been said that the specter of Dr. Helen Constance White (1896–1967) lingers in the stacks of the library. The lauded scholar broke barriers in 1936 as the first female full professor in the School of Letters and

Sciences. During an impressive career that included leadership positions in a number of different professional organizations and twenty-three honorary doctoral degrees, she also authored six novels. Standing at over six feet tall, with a penchant for plum-hued clothing, Dr. White was affectionately known as "The Purple Goddess" by her graduate students.

Many a tale has been told about the apparition of a ghostly woman clad in a lilac dress drifting through the stacks of the busy library. This specter is a helpful one, offering book suggestions to lone students by dropping the recommended book at the feet of the startled library patron. Often talked about but seldom seen, this benign spirit seems to be a welcomed addition to the library's resources.

It is not known why Dr. White roams the aisles of Memorial Library. It seems far more likely that her spirit would find a home in College Library, which is located in the hall that bears her name and houses four thousand books from her private collection. Yet sightings of this legendary professor in Memorial Library are reported year after year.

As captivating as the tales of White's ghost may be, the most frightening story about this library has nothing to do with the paranormal. The horrible reality of what happened in the library on May 2, 1979, is far more frightening than the scariest supernatural tale.

Just before midnight, a twenty-four-year-old social work student was gathering her materials in preparation to leave the small typing room where she was studying. Suddenly, the lights in the room switched off. Within moments, the student felt someone reach from behind her and put his arm around her neck. She screamed in response, and the unseen man put his hand over her mouth.

In an effort to free herself, the woman attempted to bite the man's hand, while rocking from side to side to escape his clutches. Within moments, she felt a sharp pain in her head. She had been struck on the skull with something hard. As she was beaten, she raised her arms in an effort to protect her head from the vicious blows. She continued to scream while defending herself from her unknown assailant.

In a study room on the floor below the typing room, two premed students heard the woman scream and ran to her aid. They saw twenty-five-year-old Eugene Devoe flee the typing room. In his hands was a fire axe, drenched in blood. Devoe dropped the axe. It was later discovered that he wrenched the axe from an emergency wall box in the library.

The premed students tackled Devoe, but he continued to run toward the door, dragging the men along with him. A stunned pharmacy student saw the melee and tackled Devoe, which finally brought him to the ground. Devoe was promptly arrested, and the social work student who had been wounded in the axe attack was rushed to the hospital. Fortunately, the woman lived and was later able to testify about the attack in court.

During the trial, Devoe, who was not a student at the university, offered an insanity defense, stating his "hatred (of) women" and "rejection complex" were the motives behind the brutal surprise attack. Devoe ultimately served prison time for the Memorial Library beating, but it would not be his last time assaulting a female student on campus. Years later, he was arrested on campus again for attacking another lone female student.

This terrifying true-life tale again proves that a paranormal entity is not the most frightening thing you could encounter while inside of a haunted building.

WEIRD SCIENCE

Science Hall: 550 North Park Street

The legends swirling around the Science Building are nearly as large as the five-story red brick tower that looms over Park Street. Completed in 1888 after an 1884 fire destroyed the original building, this gothic structure has housed the bodies of countless dead over the years as the location of the Department of Anatomy. Tales of the specter of a mad professor who conducted ghastly experiments in an isolated attic lab, restless spirits of misused cadavers and bodies lost in the walls are as much part of the building as its castle-like facade. Reports of disembodied footsteps and the sense that someone unseen is standing nearby are among the most frequently cited pieces of evidence of a paranormal presence in the building. While many have tried to debunk these stories, the legends live on—perhaps because there is something otherworldly in the building after all?

Until 1956, the building housed the Department of Anatomy and all the cadavers its students needed for their studies. Room 15 was used as the morgue in this era. In the period before the building was serviced by elevators, cadavers were hoisted to the fourth-floor labs by a pulley and winch system. If the rumors are true, the cadavers housed in the building were not always treated with the reverence and respect expected by those who donated their bodies to the advancement of science. Accounts of rowdy medical students driving around town with corpses in their cars and amputated fingers being hurled from the upper floors onto horrified coeds

"Science Hall" by Ryan Wick. *Licensed under CC BY 2.0.*

walking past the building have contributed to the belief that what lurks in the dark shadows of the building are the spirits of the cadavers once stored in Room 15.

Lone body parts found in unexpected places throughout this building have given credence to this theory. In 1974, students were cleaning the storage space in Room 470 when they discovered what turned out to be an embalmed human foot. The forsaken appendage, still connected to five inches of ankle bone, was slipped into a rubber rainboot for safekeeping and later returned to the medical school. During that same era, a notably long pair of human leg bones were found among the dusty discards in the fourth-floor attic. Unbelievably, the bones were again misplaced, resurfacing years later when Room 443 was being renovated.

It is not just the cadavers that are said to haunt the building. Generations of Badgers have recounted the legend of the mad professor who remains in the building where he did his greatest work. While there is evidence that the attic held private laboratories, no one knows who the mythical professor was or what type of experiments he was thought to conduct in his attic hideaway. It is said the spirit of the professor makes himself known by breaking glass.

Once, while a student was sharing the legend of the mad professor with some classmates while inside a lab in the building, the spirit put on a show for the unbelievers. During the story, glass beakers fell to the ground, one at a time, and shattered. Those who witnessed this report it was as if the beakers were dropped to the floor by an unseen hand. As well known as this legend is, many paranormal investigators have tried, and failed, to record evidence of the paranormal professor. Is the professor just a tall tale, or does his spirit still dwell in Science Hall? It is worth a visit to the red-brick building to decide for yourself.

ALL THE WORLD'S A STAGE

Wisconsin Union Theater: 800 Langdon Street

This campus landmark got its first ghost before it officially opened its doors in October 1939. During the construction of the theater, a worker fell from scaffolding and died a short time later from his injuries. The spirit of this unfortunate man is said to be one of the two spirits that haunts the Wisconsin Union Theater.

The second spirit thought to linger in the building is that of Samuel Segal, a timpanist with the Minnesota Symphony Orchestra who died onstage while performing on March 11, 1950. Segal was a last-minute replacement for the drummer who was originally scheduled to play but caught the flu. During the performance, while playing his drum, Segal suddenly fell across his instrument and then tumbled to the stage floor. As the musicians around him continued to play, Segal attempted to crawl offstage, only to collapse from the effort. The audience looked on in horror as the man was dragged backstage.

Few of the performers were aware that Segal collapsed, so the show continued while ushers quietly searched the audience for a doctor to tend to the ailing man. Sun Prairie physician Dr. Russell was soon found and rushed backstage, but it was too late for the timpanist; he was already dead.

During intermission, the orchestra manager announced to the audience that Segal died. The orchestra reconvened on stage and played Beethoven's beautiful and broody second movement of his Symphony No. 7 as a tribute to Segal. At the close of the piece, the audience rose and observed thirty seconds of silence in reverence for the loss and then quietly exited the theater. A later autopsy would reveal that Segal suffered a fatal heart attack.

Construction of the Union Theater, August 2, 1938. *University of Wisconsin-Madison Archives Collections.*

There are few who spend time in the Wisconsin Union Theater who don't believe the building is haunted. These restless spirits make themselves known through a variety of mischievous pranks. Doors seem to lock themselves, and lights are known to turn themselves on and off without human intervention, particularly in the theater's sound booth. Unexplained cold drafts swirl around the backstage area, and through the years, students and staff regularly report hearing footsteps and other sounds coming from inside the empty building. Still others have claimed to see mist-like apparitions hovering in the aisles of the theater.

Theater director Ralph Russo confirmed in a 2017 interview that the theater is haunted and shared his own spine-tingling tale of when he encountered the specter. While closing the theater in the early morning hours after a performance, he found himself alone in the building. As he made a final pass through the theater and turned out all but the aptly named "ghost light," Russo suddenly heard a tremendous crash beneath the stage, followed by a "strange shuffling" type of footstep. He initially turned to investigate but quickly changed his mind, unwilling to come face-to-face with whatever spirit was making itself known. He made a prompt exit, leaving the theater to its longtime otherworldly residents.

Renovations have done nothing to quell the paranormal activity in the building. It appears that these active ghosts feel at home in the Wisconsin Union Theater and will continue to make their presence known for generations to come.

THE FRIGHTFUL FOREST

The Arboretum: 1207 Seminole Highway, Madison

A favorite story from the Charles E. Brown collection of Wisconsin lore is that of the phantom axe man in a part of the arboretum that is now called Noe Woods. Originally a 500-acre tract of land when it was created in 1934, the property is now a sprawling 1,200 acres, dedicated to famed ecologist Aldo Leopold's plan to return the land to "original Wisconsin" plants and trees.

In Brown's tale, back when the land was still known as Bartlett's Woods, farmer Albert Lamson woke in the middle of the night to the sound of an axe blade hacking into a tree. The crack of the blade biting into the wood echoed through the quiet countryside. Despite his curiosity about the late-night lumber harvest, Lamson remained in bed. He drifted back to sleep listening to the rhythmic *whack* of the axe.

Upon rising the next morning, Lamson decided to investigate the nighttime activity in the woods. He searched high and low but could not find a single tree with as much as a nick in its bark, much less a fresh tree stump. Baffled, the farmer walked out of the woods, still thinking about the mysterious wood chopper. Then he ran into a few of his neighbors. The men were also investigating the sounds of the late-night wood harvest that woke Lamson. Despite their best efforts, the group found no evidence that there had been an axe man in the woods the night before, even though each of the men was certain he heard the distinct *crack* of a blade against the trunk of a tree.

The nocturnal wood chopping continued throughout the summer and into the fall. A group of area men joined forces to investigate the moonlight axe swinger, but attempts to find the source of the axe blows delivered under cover of night were unsuccessful. This lack of progress is more likely than not because the men would often get spooked and flee the dark woods before anything could be discovered. As the fall air turned frosty, the moonlight axe chopping ended abruptly and without explanation. This late-nineteenth-century mystery still lingers, both in the memories of family members of the people who lived through the curious events and the stories of those who recount creepy tales of happenings inside the arboretum.

In contrast, the November 2020 sounds of chopping wood were all too real when three pledges of the Chi Phi fraternal organization arrived on the property with the plan to steal a tree. The group purchased a chainsaw, rented a U-Haul and then cut down a rare, twenty-five-foot-tall Algonquin Pillar Swiss Mountain pine tree, while doing $13,000 worth of damage to the land. When the trio of nineteen-year-old criminals discovered that the theft of the rare tree was garnering a great deal of police attention, they took the stolen tree to a remote area and destroyed it in an effort to conceal their crime. The culprits were nabbed in March 2021 and later were nominally fined for the senseless destruction.

Unfortunately, the felling of trees, both real and phantom, are not the only crimes associated with this scenic property. In March 2020, a well-known doctor and her husband were found in the arboretum with gunshot wounds in the backs of their heads. Sadly, they were not the first victims of violence to be concealed on the property. The body of twenty-four-year-old Susan LeMahieu was found in April 1980, four months after she was reported missing. Many believe she was the victim of an unidentified serial killer who is suspected to be responsible for seven unsolved murders of young Madison-area women between 1968 and 1982.

Some believe these strange happenings are connected to the location of the nature preserve. There are a number of archaeological sites on the property, some of which are thought to be Ho-Chunk Nation burial mounds. Others dismiss this theory, believing it is the isolation of the area, not what has been buried in the ground, that attracts eerie events and misdeeds. Whatever the cause, it is hard to ignore that, to this day, there remains no explanation for the mysterious axe man who chopped wood all summer without felling a single tree. Maybe the land has something to do with it, after all?

SEE YOU AT THE CLUB

University Club: 803 State Street

While hardly one of the university's most haunted buildings, the University Club must be added to the list of campus locations where otherworldly events occur.

The club was founded in 1907 by university president Charles Van Hise as a faculty club. It is now one of the oldest faculty clubs in the nation. It was originally the old family home of John Barber Parkinson. In those days, the building also housed unmarried male professors. The original clubhouse was torn down in the 1920s, and the impressive Tudor-style building we know today was erected in its place.

Legend has it that the property was used as a makeshift hospital during the influenza epidemic of 1918. Perhaps that is when the building acquired the playful spirit that reportedly remains in the club. No one knows just who the spirit is or when it arrived, but it is known as Bob, and the specter makes himself known in the kitchen of the club, reminding the living that the University Club is his home—and seemingly has been for decades.

The club's former general manager, Edward Zaleski, has had firsthand experience with the impish entity. Zaleski told *Isthmus* reporter Jay Rath that during his tenure, it was not uncommon for employees to arrive at work in the morning to find every door in the kitchen wide open. Each cabinet door, each pantry door and even the refrigerator door were all open, yet no one had been in the building. With no evidence of a break-in, there were few explanations for what was happening in the kitchen that did not involve the paranormal. Employees have also encountered strange sounds and odd shadows when they are in the building alone. It may be that, once again, Bob was letting the staff know they are never really alone when they are in the University Club.

You don't have to be an employee or a club member to get the chance to experience some of the otherworldly happenings in the historic building. The club has open dining options most days, if you want to try your hand at spotting the mischievous Bob or, at least, experiencing his unseen presence.

BUCKY'S HAUNTED HOME

Camp Randal Stadium: 1440 Monroe Street

If the only thing you know about Camp Randall is the traditional playing of "Jump Around" and the cheeky chants coming from the student section, you might be surprised to learn that the stadium is considered one of the most haunted sports venues in the nation. The stadium can hold 80,321 red-and-white-clad Bucky fans. But years before the property hosted its first football game 1917, the land was the site of misery and bloodshed.

The origin of the paranormal activity is connected to how the stadium got its name. The stadium is named for Wisconsin governor Alexander Randall (1858–1861). In 1861, the Civil War began. The land that now hosts some of the rowdiest games days in the Big Ten was put into service later that year as the training grounds for an estimated seventy thousand Union Army soldiers.

Later, more than one thousand Confederate soldiers were imprisoned on the land. The conditions in Civil War prisoner of war camps were dire, and Camp Randall was no exception. The lack of adequate shelter, food and sanitation led to much suffering for the Rebel prisoners. Illnesses like

"Camp Randall Archway" by Jeff Christiansen. *Licensed under CC BY-SA 2.0.*

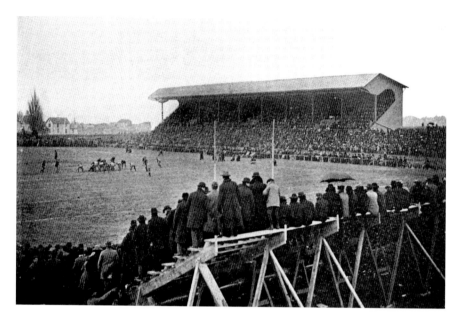

Randall Field, Wisconsin: Minnesota vs. Wisconsin, 1904. *Fielding Yost, public domain, via Wikimedia Commons.*

measles, mumps and pneumonia were a scourge in the camp. In a letter to his family, Private Paddock of the Nineteenth Wisconsin Regiment wrote of the deaths: "They die off like rotten sheep. There was 11 die off yesterday and today, and there ain't a day but what there is from two to nine dies."

The prison was eventually closed, and the remaining prisoners were transferred to Camp Douglas in Chicago, which was better equipped to house them. Those transfers came too late for the 140 Confederate soldiers who died at Camp Randall. Those 140 deceased prisoners of war are now spending the hereafter interred at the nearby Forest Hill Cemetery. They are buried in a mass grave known as Confederate Rest.

Many think the spirits of those Confederate soldiers continue to dwell on the land where they took their last breaths. Tailgaters have long claimed to see the apparitions of Confederate soldiers, still wearing their tattered rebel uniforms, near the stadium. It is not just the keg-stand crowd who have reported seeing the soldiers from beyond the grave. Over the years, there have been countless reports of sightings from the Field House and surrounding areas.

If you decide to slip out of the stadium before Bucky's fifth quarter, be on the lookout for eerie spirits of the captive Confederate soldiers, still trying to make their way home. They may be closer than you think!

CHAPTER 2

SHUDDERSOME CEMETERIES

Some people find cemeteries inherently scary places. Whether it is because they remind us of our own mortality or because the place conjures the memory of those loved and lost, graveyards can evoke strong emotions. For those who are sensitive to the paranormal, a visit to a cemetery can cause visceral reactions. Headaches, stomachaches and chills are not uncommon ways for spirits whose bodies are buried in the ground to attempt to contact the living.

If a spirit cannot physically connect from the other side, it may reveal itself in other ways. Observant graveyard visitors have been known to see unexplained shadows, strangely moving mists—even fully formed apparitions have been witnessed. If you are searching for spirits, some believe the final resting place of the dead is the right place to make that connection.

Even if you aren't seeking a connection to the spirit world, cemeteries offer wonderful insights into our history, culture and values. To inspire your next exploration of an eternal home, here are a few tales from what are considered Madison's most haunted boneyards.

THEY WATCH FROM THE SHADOWS

Orton Park: 110 Spaight Street

Have you ever felt a sense of uneasiness as you entered a location? Had a sense of dread wash over you for seemingly no reason? That very feeling is the one that those who are sensitive to the supernatural describe when they enter Orton Park.

Generations of Madisonians have gathered around the park's gazebo for festivals and music performances. Every day, kids gleefully run on the well-tended grounds and climb on the monkey bars. At first glance, it appears to be a lovely neighborhood park. And yet, for those who have a connection to the spirit world, something in the park feels very off.

That strange feeling of dread could be anchored in the past. The land that is now Orton Park was once a cemetery. When you walk through the park, you are walking over ground that once held the graves of early Madison residents. It is believed that all of the bodies were removed from the land in 1877. But were they?

In 1847, the city designated the land as a cemetery. Even then, the land was not treated as sacred. Cows regularly roamed the property, desecrating graves with their bovine hoofs as they snacked on the flowers left to honor the dead. It wasn't only animals that violated the area. Rumors persist that UW students raided a pauper's grave and stole the body to use in an anatomy class. From the little that has been recorded about the graveyard, conditions in the cemetery did not allow for a body to truly be at rest after burial.

Despite the grim circumstances in the cemetery, it filled up quickly. Madison soon had more dead than the cow-patty-dotted land could handle. As a remedy, the city opened Forest Hill Cemetery in 1857. Later, it was decided that the 256 bodies interred in the original cemetery would be exhumed and relocated to Forest Hill Cemetery.

Photo by James Steakley. *Own work, CC BY-SA 3.0, via Wikimedia Commons.*

The plan to relocate the bodies proved to be more difficult than anticipated. Many of the grave markers in the old cemetery were made of wood. Wind and rain degraded a significant number of markers, making the names painted or carved onto the wood unreadable. Errant dairy cows splintered the rotting wood as they strolled across the property. By the time plans were made to move the bodies, the graveyard had quite a number of unmarked graves.

To compound the problem, few records were kept of the burials in the graveyard, calling into question whether the claim that 256 corpses were interred on the property was accurate. Some think the number could be much higher. By 1877, it was announced that all the bodies that were once laid to rest on the land had been relocated. And yet, questions remain.

Many consider the park to be one of the most haunted places in Madison. The sensitive report feeling as if they are being watched when they visit Orton Park. Many have shared accounts of seeing flickering shadows that linger behind the tree line. These shadowy figures seem to follow those who have spotted them as they walk through the park.

Perhaps most eerie is the belief that the spirits in the park somehow inhabit the trees. The trees that loom over the pathway in the park have repelled the sensitive for years. Some sense an unearthly aura coming from the trees. On a stormy day, when the wind is roaring, the trees groan and creak in a way that could turn a skeptic into a true believer.

Do these strange happenings occur because there are long-forgotten bodies buried on the land? Could it be the spirits that linger in Orton Park are the dead who chose to remain in the final burial spot they chose for themselves? Whatever the reason these spirits remain, they are one of the park's most popular hidden attractions. If you do your own ghost hunting in the park, remember that with each step you take, you are likely walking on a grave site.

Whether that grave is empty or not—well, that is anyone's guess.

Madison's Most Famous (and Famously Haunted) Cemetery

Forest Hill Cemetery: 1 Speedway Road

Legend has it that Forest Hill Cemetery is Madison's most haunted cemetery. Just who haunts this historic cemetery, and why do the spirits linger here? These questions have no clear-cut answers. Curious ghost hunters have been

A quiet afternoon at Forest Hill Cemetery. *Anna Lardinois.*

drawn to the property for generations, yet the mystery remains. While there is no consensus about what is happening inside the graveyard, all agree that something supernatural is attached to this land.

Long before Forest Hill Cemetery was established, Madison's early settlers were buried on what is now known as Bascom Hill. The city then established a graveyard in 1847 on the isthmus, in what is now known as Orton Park. Soon, Madison's growth made it necessary for the city to acquire a larger tract of land to hold its dead. The 140-acre cemetery was established in 1857. It is the final resting place of eight Wisconsin governors and some of Madison's most influential historical figures.

While no one knows why Forest Hill Cemetery is so famously haunted, there are a few popular theories. One suggests that some of the spirits spending their afterlife in the cemetery feel unsettled because their graves are not properly marked. There are hundreds of unmarked graves on the property. It is estimated that there are as many as 339—or maybe even more—graves without markers or with markers so eroded by time that their inscriptions have vanished. Some believe that the spirits of those buried deep in the earth without a marker to acknowledge their time among the living cannot rest peacefully. Might these souls find peace if their names were known to all who passed by their graves?

Others attribute the presence of paranormal activity to the number of reinterred bodies that found a second or even a third "final" resting place inside the bucolic cemetery. Many of the unmarked graves are thought to be those of early Madison settlers who were first buried in one of the town's early cemeteries. The belief is that when these bodies were disinterred, the spirits connected to the unearthed corpses were no longer at peace. Bodies that were once laid to rest beside loved ones in family plots were reburied in Forest Hill Cemetery alone and stripped of their identity. Perhaps these spirits roam in search of those they once knew and loved, longing to rest beside them again?

Another persistent but outmoded theory is that the supernatural activity inside the cemetery is connected to the area's earliest inhabitants. At some time between 500 and 1000 CE, during the Late Woodland Period, Native Americans used the land to bury their dead. This is evidenced by the four effigy mounds that remain on the property. These mounds were used to entomb leaders and warriors of the community. Visitors will find one linear mound, two panther mounds and a goose mound on the grounds. The head of the goose mound was destroyed by railroad development in the 1880s. Unfortunately, the other mounds that were once built on the land have been destroyed. Some believe the mounds are linked to mystical spiritual powers. Others find that belief culturally offensive. You can see these historically significant formations in sections 15 and 35 of the cemetery. Could there be something about this land that drew two different cultures from different historical eras to use it as a place to honor their dead?

Those looking for a less mystical explanation for restless spirits may find answers in section 34 of the cemetery. Known as the Soldiers' Lot, the area contains the graves of those lost in the Civil War, as well as the Spanish-American War and World War I. It is the graves of the soldiers who fell during the war between the North and South that claim the most paranormal attention.

There are both 240 Union soldiers and 140 Confederate soldiers buried in the cemetery. The Rebel soldiers met their ends while being held as prisoners of war at Camp Randall. Many claim the apparitions of those men who succumbed to hardship and disease while imprisoned still roam the city. Do the spirits of these men, bitter enemies in life, bristle at the proximity of their foes to their final resting places?

Amid the interred soldiers lie the bodies of eight children. These children died while in the care of the Soldiers' Orphan Home. The home cared for the children of Union soldiers orphaned during the war. The children,

Forest Hill Cemetery Chapel. *Anna Lardinois.*

buried together among the soldiers' graves, finally received a grave marker in 1873. Might the spirits of Union men brought home for burial seek out the children they left behind?

Ghostly sightings of soldiers, whom many have reported seeing both in the graveyard and in the area around Camp Randall, are a frequent occurrence. Those who have a sensitivity to paranormal experiences have reported a number of distressing happenings as they walk through the Forest Hill Cemetery. They report being overwhelmed by emotions, describing feelings of deep sorrow and a dreadful sinking feeling in the pits of their stomachs. Others have experienced physical sensations, like headaches and stomachaches, particularly in the section where the soldiers are buried. These physical and emotional sensations have been attributed to the number of unseen entities that roam the graveyard.

The land has been used to bury the dead for over one thousand years, and it is linked it to generations of love and loss. What causes the restlessness of the spirits of those buried there may forever be a mystery, at least until we join the spirits on the other side. The only certainty seems to be that whatever lingers on the land has likely been there for quite some time, and it shows no sign of moving on.

THE ANSWER IS BURIED IN SECTION H

Resurrection Cemetery: 2705 Regent Street

Directly across the street from Forest Hill Cemetery is Resurrection Cemetery. This graveyard is run by the Catholic Diocese of Madison. It was formed in 1949, when Holy Cross Cemetery and Calvary Cemetery were combined to create Resurrection Cemetery.

There are many notable people who are spending their afterlife on the Resurrection grounds. Interred there are three Madison bishops and a number of priests. Beloved comedian Chris Farley, of *Saturday Night Live* fame, is entombed in the chapel mausoleum. Politicians, business owners and even a few criminals are spending eternity, side by side, on the land.

Like most cemeteries, legends of hauntings swirl around this final resting place. The sensitive report a feeling of uneasiness as they move through the forty-acre property. Visitors have felt cold spots while walking among the earlier gravestones. Some of those same people have caught sight of shadowy figures flitting between the monuments out of the corners of

Chapel Mausoleum. *Anna Lardinois.*

their eyes. As intriguing as these paranormal happenings are, they pale in comparison to an unsolved mystery whose final chapter is buried deep beneath the hallowed grounds.

Perhaps the most talked-about person laid to rest in the cemetery is a little girl who lived over a century ago. Her grave is in section H of Resurrection Cemetery. This seven-year-old was laid to rest in what was Calvary Cemetery on Monday, September 11, 1911. More than one hundred years later, Madisonians continue to be troubled, and fascinated, by the mysterious death of the child.

Anna Marie Lemberger, forever remembered by history as "Little Annie," was born in 1904. She was one of Martin and Magdaline Lemberger's five children. The family lived in Madison's Greenbush neighborhood, which, despite being only six blocks from the state capital and three blocks away from the university, was a neighborhood plagued with crime and poverty. The Lembergers' home was on South Frances Street, near where the Kohl Center stands today.

Shortly after five in the morning on September 6, 1911, it was discovered that little Annie was taken from her bed sometime in the night. The open window in her bedroom gave the sole indication of where the child had gone. The only thing missing from the room, besides Annie, was the white nightgown the child wore to bed. The police were called, and soon all of Madison began a frenzied search for the girl.

The story of the missing girl quickly made national news, and newspapers around the country breathlessly reported on the search. Back in Madison, it seemed that everyone was a potential suspect. Prayer vigils were held at St. James, where the girl attended school, and groups of concerned neighbors scoured the area looking for traces of the child. Each day that passed without the discovery of the girl put more pressure on an already tense town.

On September 9, hopes were dashed when the body of the little girl was pulled from Brittingham Bay on Lake Monona. The child was found naked and had bruising on the left side of her head. It was later revealed that the girl did not have any water in her lungs and had likely died of suffocation. Little Annie had been discarded in the lake after she died. The anxiety the town felt for the missing girl was quickly replaced by rage against the unknown person who ended her life.

The city was devastated by the discovery and vowed to find the murderer. Meanwhile, the child was laid to rest on September 11. Her funeral was attended by thousands, and the mournful ceremony made the front page of every major Wisconsin newspaper. When her body was lowered into the ground on that warm autumn day, the mystery of what happened to Annie was far from over. It many ways, it had just begun.

Madison's Mayor Schubert offered a $1,000 reward for the capture of the murderer. Madisonians didn't need a financial incentive to search for the child murderer; they were fueled by rage. The town wanted the killer off their streets and was willing to resort to vigilante justice to ensure that would happen.

Suspicion soon fell on neighborhood ne'er-do-well Jack A. Johnson. Known locally as "Dogskin," because he had once stolen the tanned hide of a dog, Johnson fit the bill. He lived near the Lemberger home, had a history of inappropriate behavior with young girls and had spent time in the state mental asylum. His family gave him an alibi, but it didn't impress the mobs looking for justice for Annie.

Johnson was arrested as an angry crowd called for his blood. He confessed to the crime. But he later recanted, claiming he only confessed to be taken into custody so he would not fall into the hands of the violent mob, who were willing to take the law into their own hands. Johnson remained in police custody, but soon, some would begin to accuse a person who had far more access to Annie than Johnson. The finger of blame for the murder was pointed at Martin Lemberger, Annie's own father. Despite the rumors flying around town, Johnson was ultimately convicted of the murder of the girl. For ten years, Johnson sat in prison, and townspeople whispered gossip that Martin Lemberger got away with murder.

In 1921, Johnson appeared in court in a bid to win his freedom. During the trial, a surprise witness appeared on the stand whose testimony would change the course of events. Mae Sorenson, a neighbor of both Johnson and Lemberger, appeared before the court and testified that Alois, Annie's brother, told her their father killed Annie in a drunken rage. She also claimed that Martin discovered what the boy told her, and threatened to choke her if she told anyone. This salacious story put Annie's murder once again on the front pages of newspapers across the country.

From there, the tale spiraled into several different court cases, each with conflicting testimony. The result was years of legal battles. Eventually, Johnson won his freedom and ultimately received compensation from the state for false imprisonment.

Mae Sorenson was branded a liar by Madisonians, and to this day, it is believed by many that she was paid for her testimony. This is an accusation she always denied. Martin Lumberger never faced murder charges, but he lived in the shadow of suspicion for the remainder of his days. Later, Magdaline would successfully sue a media outlet for writing that Martin was a murderer. She used money awarded by the court to buy the monument that marks Little Annie's grave in section H of Resurrection Cemetery.

Resurrection Cemetery. *Anna Lardinois.*

All the those involved in this sensational crime are now dead, but the mystery of who killed Annie lives on. Martin and Magadeline Lumberger are interred in Resurrection Cemetery, next to their little girl who never had the chance to grow up. Annie is buried near the man who either took her life or whose life was burdened by the painful loss of a child coupled with the suspicion that he caused that loss.

Across the street, in section 23 of Forest Hill Cemetery, lies the body of Dogskin Johnson, a man who was either falsely accused of a crime and had ten years of his life stolen or a child murderer who paid a light penalty for his terrible crime. Just one section over from Johnson, in section 22, lies Mae Sorenson, a woman who either took money to free a killer or whose refusal to tell what she knew cost a man ten years of his life.

The murder of Little Annie Lumberger is one of Wisconsin's most famous cold cases, and it intrigues modern sleuths every bit as much as it did those who hunted for the girl a century ago. Annie's story has been recounted in a number of books and countless websites. Cold-case crackers have posed theories and compiled evidence, but the answer to who killed Annie remains a mystery.

The truth died long ago and is now buried on both sides of Speedway Road, never to be revealed.

CHAPTER 3

THEY ARE HERE FOR THE BOO-ze

Time and time again, Wisconsin tops the list of the nation's drunkest states. Given our love of the sauce, it is not a surprise that Madison ghost fans often like to seek out spirits while sipping on spirits. There may be no better place to pursue the supernatural than the bars and restaurants in the Madison area. Here are just a few of the many spooky spots where you can find ghosts and grub. Or specters and shots. Either way, you'll find both boos and booze at all of these spook-tacular establishments.

ODD OCCURRENCES AT THE OHIO

Ohio Tavern: 224 Ohio Street

Tucked into the Atwood neighborhood is a brick structure built in 1913 that was originally used as a bank. The building was converted into a tavern in 1933 and is now one of Madison's oldest licensed bars. Instantly recognizable for its glowing neon Blatz sign, the Ohio Tavern has been embraced by generations of dive bar enthusiasts. The relaxed atmosphere and budget-friendly prices keep the bar filled with regulars. And, it seems, some of those regulars like the Ohio Tavern so much, they decided that they'd never leave. Ever.

The historic dive's former owner, Terre Sims, knew the place was haunted before she signed her name to the deed in 1993. The ghost greeted her

Ohio Tavern's beloved Blatz sign. *Anna Lardinois.*

with what would become a regular occurrence behind the bar, the flinging open of cabinet doors by an unseen hand. Far from being frightened, the paranormal enthusiast was curious to learn more about the spirits that dwelled in the Ohio Tavern. Sims began to catalog and share the ghostly happenings in her building. Before long, she discovered she wasn't the only one who sensed spirits in the building. Her employees and customers had supernatural experiences in the bar as well.

The barroom spirits seemed to be playful ones. They liked to clink the glasses in the bar when the room was empty and still. Sometimes, they'd move balls on the pool tables. Occasionally, objects would be tossed off shelves behind the bar by an undetected entity. Employees and patrons alike would feel something unseen brush up against them and, every now and then, feel a gentle but insistent touch on their arm or shoulder from an invisible hand. Based on the tales, these spirits did not frighten people; they just seemed to want to let the living know they were present, even if they could not be seen.

Sims is quoted as saying she thought there might be as many as five ghosts lingering in the building. While the spirits that made themselves known in the barroom seemed to like interacting with people during business hours, the supernatural activity never ceased. Spirits were active in the building both day and night. During her time as the owner of the bar, it was common to hear disembodied footsteps throughout the building.

The old basement, with its low ceilings and thick stone walls, would likely awaken fear in anyone, even if it wasn't rumored to be haunted. The eerie-looking jumble of rooms seemed to be a hot spot for paranormal activity. Employees who went into the basement reported the sense of being watched from the dark corners of the underground room. Unexplained shadows moved across the walls, and sometimes, the entity would get physical with the employees. Two female bartenders, both with long, blond hair, felt an unseen hand tug their tresses at the bottom of the creaky basement stairs. No one who needed to be in the basement would stay very long.

Perhaps whatever dwelled in the basement did not want to stay there. Both employees and patrons have reported that the heavy basement door will open and close itself, despite being latched shut!

Sims felt certain the apartment above the bar, where she and her husband lived, was also haunted. Her husband was skeptical that a specter inhabited their apartment—until the pair awoke to an unnerving scene. Every door in the apartment was wide open, including the oven door, the refrigerator door and the doors of all the cupboards. The couple were alone in the locked apartment when this happened. While Sims's husband had dismissed her earlier reports of spirit activity, like phantom knocks on the apartment door, this dramatic display was much harder to dismiss. Based on the circumstances, it seemed that an otherworldly occurrence was the most likely explanation for the strange happening.

Who are the spirits at the Ohio and why do they remain in the tavern? That's anyone's guess. It is rumored that a tenant in the upper apartment hanged himself sometime during the 1940s, which could explain some of the spiritual energy in the building. Sims theorized that some of the spirits in the tavern are the ghosts of former factory workers who were regulars when the Ohio was their neighborhood watering hole. She dubbed the most active spirit in the bar Ollie. She sensed this spirit was a short man in bib overalls who had a penchant for Old Style Beer. This spirit appeared to have a favorite barstool, the second from the end of the bar. It was Ollie's spot, and he'd often swivel the seat of the stool to get a little attention. Countless people have claimed to see his stool spinning around without any earthly intervention.

Sims was so curious about her ghosts that she invited the television show *Paranormal Generation* to conduct an investigation of the building in 2011.

Four investigators, led by Curt Strutz, loaded their equipment into the Ohio Tavern, focusing their search on the barroom and basement of the building. Despite their best efforts, they could not get the spirits to interact with them. While the program is no longer on the air, the episode can be seen on the internet.

Did Sims take the spirits with her when the bar changed hands in 2016? The new owners have not added any new tales to the bar's often-told lore. Today those seeking tacos and karaoke outnumber the ghost hunters at the bar, but that does not mean restless spirits don't continue to roam the historic building. If you go to the Ohio, perhaps the spirits might interact with you, if you ask them nicely.

If you believe the lore about the historic bar, one thing seems certain: last call is a warning that only pertains to the living when you're at the Ohio Tavern.

Where the Underworld and the Otherworld Meet

Wonder Bar: 222 E. Olin Avenue

The Wonder Bar embraces its reputation as a haunted bar, but it truly celebrates its mobster past. Originally opened in 1929 by Chicago-based mobster Roger "the Terrible" Touhy and his brother Eddie, it is thought to have been built to launder money and aid in the family's bootlegging operation. Roger Touhy, a Capone rival, is best known for the kidnapping of John Factor, the brother of cosmetics mogul Max Factor. His mobbed-up brother Eddie ran the bar, and it quickly became a remote, northern retreat for big-city mobsters who were looking to take a break from police raids and FBI surveillance.

The building boasts a list of former patrons that reads like a who's who of midwestern mobsters. Among those who enjoyed the hospitality at Wonder Bar are John Dillinger, Al Capone, and Baby Face Nelson. The bar was designed the serve a rough-and-tumble clientele. The stone-constructed building is a striking one. It is flanked by turrets, which were built with notches. The notches allowed the mobsters inside to ease the barrels of their Tommy guns out of the building, making it easier to shoot any intruders foolish enough to take on the Touhy brothers or their cronies.

Legend has it that the former owner, Eddie, may be buried behind the second-floor fireplace. He mysteriously disappeared in the early 1950s and

Age: 44(42) Height:5.53/4 Weight: 139   Hair:Ches.Dk.&Gr Eyes: Yel.Lt.Bl.Sl.Comp: Medium
Nat'y:IllinoiRec'd: 2-24-34 From: Cook County   Crime: Kid.Ran.Sent: 99 yrs. FBI:
Occupation: Electrician   (Description taken 2-26-34) (Picture taken. 7-30-41)

Noticeable markings (face): Raised lump $\frac{1}{2}$ x $\frac{1}{2}$—3/4
Below center left jaw on neck. Light mole $\frac{1}{4}$ to
right just below right wing of nose.
Others: III. Nose turns slightly to left.
Lower lip turns under.

Wire information to
E.M. STUBBLEFIELD, WARDEN.
ILLINOIS STATE PENITENTIARY
JOLIET, ILLINOIS.

Roger "the Terrible" Touhy. *Public domain.*

was never seen again. When Eddie could not be found, wise guys began to speculate that Eddie might be right under their noses. Literally. While the fireplace has never been dismantled or examined in an attempt to find the body, the persistent rumor has been told so often it is now accepted as fact.

If it is true that Eddie met a violent end and is now bricked into the walls of the building, we know his brother Roger didn't fare much better. Roger was murdered on his sister's doorstep in 1959, less than a month after being released from a twenty-six-year stint in the big house for the Factor kidnapping. To this day, many Touhy supporters still believe the kidnapping rap was a frame-up, and they blame Roger's conviction and eventual execution on the Chicago Outfit, once led by his bitter rival, Al Capone.

In addition to the tales about mobsters and their molls are the stories of paranormal happenings in the storied steakhouse. As with many haunted locations, there have been countless reports of items moving around the bar by an unseen hand. In another bar, a mischievous spirit that moves object would be a key draw, but not at the Wonder Bar. Ghost enthusiasts pile into the restaurant in hopes of encountering an apparition.

Two otherworldly entities are regularly seen in the building. The identity of both spirits remains a mystery. One apparition appears in the form of a man wearing a fedora and trench coat. The figure lurks around the staircase leading to the second floor of the building. Because of his clothing, many think he may have met some rough mob justice in the building, causing his spirit to linger in the building where his life was snuffed out.

The other ghostly figure spotted in the Wonder Bar is a beautiful redhead, thought to be the same woman who is depicted in a pinup-style painting that has hung in the bar for years. There is much debate about who this stunner is, but her slinky apparition—and the sound of her laughter—reportedly remains in the building where her sultry portrait still hangs.

The basement seems to be a key source of activity. People report hearing disembodied footsteps walking down the stairs into the basement, muffled voices and sound of doors violently slamming. The subterranean rooms, which once had tunnels that led toward Lake Mendota to aid in bootlegging activities, are thought to have been a place where many a mobster received retribution for missteps. It is not known whether anyone died in the basement, but it seems certain that the basement saw more than its share of bloodshed and evil deeds over the years.

If you are looking for a good steak, a stiff drink, midwestern mafia memorabilia and titillating tales of the paranormal, Madison's Wonder Bar is the only place you can find it all.

A Haunting on the Half Shell

Tempest Oyster Bar: 120 E Wilson Street

The living and the dead have mingled at the brick Georgian Revival on Wilson Street since the building was completed in 1929. It was built to serve both as an apartment building and a funeral parlor. Frautschi Funeral Home served generations of Madisonians, preparing bodies for the afterlife from 1929 to 1971. The ground floor of the building, which played host to countless wakes, is now the location of Madison's most celebrated seafood restaurant, Tempest Oyster Bar.

Since the restaurant's opening in 2011, it has continually appeared on lists of Madison's most haunted establishments. Reports of the paranormal activities in the building are often vague but are so intriguing that a local ghost tour company makes this restaurant a key stop on their tour. Cold spots, items moving without earthly intervention and locked doors opening seemingly on their own are reported in this storied building.

It seems not all the spirit activity in the building can be attributed to those whose bodies have passed through the funeral parlor. In 1997, a man hanged himself in the basement. Some believe the spiritual energy of this troubled soul lingers in the area where the body was discovered. The room where the death occurred is notably colder than the other basement rooms. Those who have visited claim to feel a sense of uneasiness inside the room. Whether this emotional response is due to residual spiritual energy or the result of visiting a space where a tragedy occurred has is anyone's guess. But it seems worthy of some paranormal investigation.

If you are out on the town and your evening in Madison demands both oysters and otherworldly experiences, the Tempest is the only place to go!

The Ghostly Great Dane

The Great Dane: 123 East Doty Street

Great Dane Pub & Brewing Company is not afraid of its ghostly reputation; instead, it shines a spotlight on its otherworldly occupants. The brewpub, opened in 1994, is housed in a brick Queen Anne–style building built in 1854. As one of Madison's oldest remaining buildings, the structure is steeped in the history of the capital city. And, it seems, part of history still remains in the building, in the form of ghostly activity.

Paranormal encounters are par for the course for the employees working at the Great Dane. In a 2021 interview with the Milwaukee CBS affiliate WDJT, manager Molly Conkey said the spirits began to reveal themselves to her just a few weeks after she started working at the brewpub. Late one night, she was doing her closing paperwork and she heard a man whisper, "What time is it?" When she turned around to answer the man, she found she was alone in the room. That was her first ghostly encounter at the pub—but hardly her last.

Perhaps the spirit who whispered to Molly is the same ghostly man who has been seen walking up the back stairs of the brewpub? The solid-looking apparition has been spotted on the staircase many times. Each time he is confronted by an employee for being in a restricted area, he suddenly vanishes without a trace. The man's identity, and what he is trying to reach at the top of the staircase, continues to be a mystery.

Another employee tale that continues to send shivers down the spines of those who visit the Great Dane happened late one night in the pool room. The often-repeated, eerie tale is that of two employees who were in the building alone, late one night. They heard a crash in the pool room, so they went to investigate. Their attention was drawn to a row of pool cues secured in a rack mounted to the wall. The employees stood dumbfounded as they watched the pool cues drop to the floor. It was as if an unseen hand was removing the cues from the rack and dropping them to the floor, one by one. The clatter echoed throughout the empty building as each cue

Built in 1854, this is one of Madison's oldest buildings. *Anna Lardinois.*

struck the floor. What they saw shocked them and remains unexplained to this day.

It is possible that the origins of the haunting go back to the time when the building was the Fess Hotel. Established by the Fess family in 1858 and active until the 1970s, the hotel was one of the first in Madison. Tens of thousands of visitors have walked through its doors, from esteemed government officials to ladies of the evening and just about everyone else who passed through Madison. While the clientele changed as the neighborhood changed, one thing was constant for years: the hotel did not sell liquor.

The Fess family were supporters of the temperance movement, and their hotel was patronized by those who wanted to see the country go dry. In 1901, America's most famous anti-alcohol crusader, Carrie Nation, stayed in the hotel when she visited Madison. With the building's notoriously dry roots, it stands to reason that any spirits that remain from that time do not approve of the consumption of alcohol. Could it be the beer that flows freely from the brewpub's taps that keeps the spirits in the building active? Is their disapproval of the consumption of the giggle juice preventing them from experiencing a restful afterlife? That is certainly one theory.

Alcohol might cause ire in teetotalling spirits, but that is not the only thing amiss in the brewpub. While the origins of these eerie happenings are unknown, something strange is happening in the aptly titled "spooky room" in the basement. Though it is off-limits during regular hours, the brewpub allows a local ghost tour company to bring their groups down the stairs of the century-old building to experience the dreaded room for themselves. It is rumored to be unnaturally cold, and visitors often report feeling an overwhelming sense of dread upon entering the room. It is said no one choses to linger any longer than necessary in the unnerving room.

The building on Doty Street is a piece of Madison history. And so are its longtime otherworldly residents. Belly up to the bar and explore this history. Whether you seek brews or boos, the Great Dane has it.

Putting the Boo in Baraboo

Old Baraboo Inn: 135 Walnut Street, Baraboo

Just a stone's throw outside Madison is a bar that some say is one of the most haunted buildings in all of Wisconsin. Many businesses rumored to be haunted fervently deny it, but Old Baraboo Inn is not one of those places.

Old Baraboo Inn is considered one of the most haunted buildings in Wisconsin. *"Count Me Inn" by Panhandle Prince. Licensed under CC BY-NC-SA 2.0.*

This haunting is so well known that the bar has been featured on the Food Network's *10 Most Haunted Restaurants in America* and the Travel Channel's *Hometown Horror.* The owners have embraced the things that go bump in the night by offering frequent ghost tours and what they report was the world's largest ghost hunt back in September 2017.

The brick building, once known as the Bender Hotel, was completed in 1879 and began as a boardinghouse. The business later diversified to offer some more scandalous services; it's served as a roadhouse, a brothel and a honky-tonk bar during its more than a century of use. It was ideally located across from the small town's railway station, and business boomed during the era when rail transportation was the best way for travelers to cover long distances. Abandoned for more than a decade, the building was renovated by B.D. Farr and is now a popular bar and grill.

It appears that most of hauntings in this building are connected to an era when the Old Baraboo Inn was a rough and rollicking place where a number of people lost their lives. The otherworldly party continues; some hear honky-tonk piano music pouring from the empty barroom. Supernatural revelers have been spotted in the bar as well.

With feathers in her hair, a good-time girl from the other side of the veil still can be seen shimmying across the dance floor—that is, if the jukebox plays her favorite song. She is dressed in red, and a number of people throughout the years have claimed to see the ghostly woman clad in saloon girl attire in the bar. She is thought to come from the era when the building was a brothel. The apparition of the former lady of the night, dubbed Mary by a modern patron, is the most popular of the spirits that have made the Old Baraboo Inn their home. Many believe the often-seen Mary is a former prostitute who bled to death in the building in 1903.

Paranormal activity in the building is not limited to appearances by former ladies of the evening. Those who work in the kitchen claim to have repeatedly dodged flying dishes and other cookware thrown by an unseen hand. Both employees and patrons have experienced doors opening and closing without earthly aid. In a terrifying turn, owner B.C. Farr has stated that if the entity lingering in this area is displeased with an employee, it has been known to shut the door of the walk-in cooler located in the basement while the employee is working in there—and then shut off the lights, leaving the frightened staff member trembling in the dark.

It's not just the bar and kitchen that have reported paranormal happenings; tenants in the second-floor apartments have also reported eerie experiences. Those staying in the upper units have reported hearing their name spoken by the voice of an unseen woman. They have reported objects moved around the rooms without earthly intervention and have been bothered by unexplained sounds of tapping and knocking.

While residents find this otherworldly activity unsettling, guests in the bar and restaurant cannot get enough of the supernatural events. These days, the Old Baraboo Inn invites paranormal enthusiasts to experience these eerie happenings for themselves by attending one of its scheduled ghost hunts and tours.

CHAPTER 4
MADISON'S MOST FAMOUS

Named for James Madison, the nation's fourth president, Wisconsin's capital city is the second-largest city in the state. Nestled between four lakes, Madison is a beautiful place, and it's home to Bucky and the University of Wisconsin. It is also home to some of the strangest, most talked-about haunted locations in Wisconsin. Perhaps the best place to explore some of the city's most famous hauntings is at the heart of the city, Capitol Square.

FORWARD!

Wisconsin State Capitol: 2 East Main Street

Wisconsin has had five capitol buildings, and three of them were built in Madison. In 1837, the first stones were laid on the Madison capitol grounds. Just five years later, blood would stain the floor of the historic building. It was the first blood that was shed in the building, but it would not be the last.

In 1842, in a room full of politicians, a murder was committed on the legislature floor. It was during a session on February 11, when James Russell Vineyard, a Democratic politician representing Grant County, was arguing over the appointment of the Grant County sheriff with fellow statesman Charles C.P. Arndt, a Whig who represented a notable portion of the eastern part of the state. Tempers on both sides were still flaring when the meeting was adjourned. An angry Arndt rose from his desk and stormed over to Vineyard. The pair exchanged bitter words. Eyewitnesses saw Arndt strike Vineyard in the face. To the shock of everyone in the room, Vineyard drew his gun. Before anyone could stop him, Vineyard shot Arndt, in clear view of the politicians lingering in the room.

The wounded Whig spun around from the impact of the shot and then stumbled about, clutching the left side of his chest. Minutes later, Arndt was dead. Fans of macabre history can see the vest Arndt was killed in, complete with the tattered bullet hole and bloodstains, on display at the Wisconsin Historical Museum.

As expected, Vineyard was immediately arrested. The headline-making murder shocked the nation. Vineyard was later returned to his home district to be tried for the killing in the capitol. To the dismay of many Wisconsinites, Vineyard was acquitted of manslaughter and even went on to serve as a state assemblyman in 1849. But many believe the tale of that fateful day does not end here.

Legend has it that Arndt still roams the land where his blood was spilled. The building where he was murdered no longer stands. It was eventually deemed too small for the needs of the growing government and replaced with a domed building that was constructed between 1857 and 1869. They say the destruction of the first capitol building on that property did not chase away the angry spirit of Arndt. The politician's body lies in Green Bay, but his ire still remains in Madison. It is said the spirit of the murdered man can be felt as unexpected cold spots throughout the current building.

Sadly, Arndt's murder was not the last violent death to occur in the capitol and leave a ghostly legacy. The next tragedy that befell the land is connected to the second capitol building. That building also became too small for Wisconsin's needs, and the structure was being expanded when blood was spilled on the land once again.

It was shortly after one thirty in the afternoon on November 8, 1883, when a tremendous crash was heard throughout Madison. The rolling rumble from the crash lasted for more than thirty seconds, and the sound could be heard from more than two miles away. When the crashing subsided, it was replaced by screams of terror and moans of pain. As pleas for help filled the air, a vast cloud of dust rose over the capitol building. As the airborne debris began to settle over the city, Madisonians were horrified to discover what had happened. The south wing of the capitol building had collapsed.

The cries for help were coming from inside the building. Buried beneath the rubble were plasterers, masons, carpenters and other construction workers who

The former state capitol that burned in 1904. *Public domain.*

had been toiling on the south wing of the building when the pillars supporting the construction swung out, causing the south wall to fall. Moments later, the roof caved in, trapping workers inside. Chaos erupted as all three stories of the wing collapsed, trapping an unknown number of workmen inside the structurally unstable building.

A hook-and-ladder team rushed to the building to recover the men trapped inside. The *Chicago Tribune* reported on November 9 that rescuers were horrified to see about a dozen workmen "hanging by their legs from some of the upper rafters, which were attached to the side walls and did not fall. They became entrapped in this painful position, though flying debris had killed two or three and relieved them from their torture." Other men were buried under more than ten feet of crushed stone and splintered wood.

The rescue took hours, and in the end, five men died in the ruins of the south wing. Nineteen men were seriously injured in the collapse, many of them so severely that it was believed their deaths were imminent. It took time, but all the bodies were recovered from the property. But that does not mean their spirits left the scene of the accident. It is believed that the south wing of the capitol is now the most haunted area of the

The current capitol building for the state of Wisconsin. *Public domain*.

The rotunda of the capitol building. *Anna Lardinois*.

building. There are countless reports of doors opening themselves and then slamming shut without human intervention. Throughout the years, employees have claimed to hear the heavy tread of work boots plodding down empty hallways. The ghostly footfalls echo in the stillness, sending shivers down the spines of all who hear it.

The second capitol, where this horrible accident occurred, burned to the ground in 1904 when the flame from a gaslight ignited a newly varnished ceiling. The blaze raged on for seventeen hours, and when the flames finally died, there was little left of the once-grand building. No lives were lost in the fire, but the flames did not rid the land of the spirits that continue to dwell there.

The capitol building that stands today is Madison's third. Guests are welcome to tour the building during regular business hours. Inside, you'll see a great deal of Wisconsin history. And, if you are lucky—or very unlucky, depending on your desire for a paranormal experience—you just might experience a few spooky things that don't appear on the self-guided tour maps.

MYSTICAL PICNIC POINT

Lakeshore Nature Preserve: 2000 University Bay Drive

If you ask around Madison for a list of spooky locations, chances are you'll hear that there are witches on Picnic Point. The thought of witches might conjure images of bubbling cauldrons and late-night rituals, but you won't find that type of witches on Lake Medota's south shore. Rather than a tale rooted in the occult, the legend of the Picnic Point witches is part of Ho-Chunk folklore.

Historian and folklorist Charles E. Brown recorded the tale of the Picnic Points witches as it was told to him by Mrs. Anna White Wings. The tale was passed down through generations of Ho-Chunk, and Brown preserved the tale at the Wisconsin Historical Society to ensure the story remained part of Madison history.

According to the tale, happy Ho-Chunk families were living on Picnic Point. Their tranquility was disturbed by witches who swept into the community and snatched their children, only to eat them later. The now-childless parents pleaded with the spirit Earthmaker, or Man'una, to help them. The Ho-Chuck Creator God returned the children to their mourning

Picnic Point, Lake Mendota. Madison, Wisconsin

A scenic postcard of the lovely Picnic Point. *J.A. Fagan Publishing, Madison, Wisconsin. Public domain, via Wikimedia Commons.*

parents and punished the witches for their misdeed by turning them into hackberry trees.

The witches were condemned to an eternity of being rooted in Picnic Point, feeding their berries to the families whose children they once tried to eat. Those who visit the land can still find traces of the witches. A careful look at the hackberry trees on Picnic Point will reveal tiny black "hairs" growing from their branches. These hairs are a telltale sign that the hackberry trees were once witches. The imprisoned witches still make themselves known on the peninsula; when the branches of the gnarled trees are whipped by storm winds, the witches can be heard groaning in protest.

The witches of the Point are legendary, but they are not howling in the wind alone; a famous ghost may have joined them. He is German-born architect August Kurtzbock, who designed many of early Madison's most prominent buildings. He had his hand in Wisconsin's second capitol building and Madison's first city hall and first synagogue, as well as other notable buildings. While despondent over a downturn in his formerly illustrious career, Kurtzbock drowned himself off Picnic Point on November 1, 1868. There are those who claim that the architect's spirit rises from the lake in a misty swirl, then drifts toward Capitol Square, the former location of one of his most celebrated creations.

Whether it is through folklore or ghostly tales, storytellers have left their mark on the mile-long peninsula since humans first visited Picnic Point at least twelve thousand years ago. The land contains six story-filled effigy mounds and countless tales that continue to captivate eager listeners.

Haunts on the Hill?

Sanatorium Hill: 1202 Northport Drive

Sanitorium Hill exists because tuberculous, the scourge of the early twentieth century, visited Madison. Countless Madisonians were stricken with this highly contagious airborne disease that was marked by a chronic cough, fever, rapid weight loss and night sweats. Sufferers were plagued with mucous-filled lungs. The thick white phlegm expectorated by the bone-rattling coughs of the afflicted earned the disease the terrifying moniker the "White Plague." The persistent coughing damaged the sufferer's airways, making it common for the ill to cough up blood. A blood-sprayed handkerchief was often a telltale indication that someone was infected with tuberculous. It was a terrifying disease with no known cure; at the turn of the century, 450 Americans died every day from tuberculous.

The highly contagious nature of the disease led to the development of sanatoriums. These treatment centers were most often located in rural, isolated areas. Sanatoriums served to not only protect the general population from catching the infection but also to provide the ample fresh air it was believed the afflicted needed to recover from the dreaded disease. Madison's Lake View Tuberculosis Sanatorium opened in 1930. Perched on Dane County's second-highest point, the imposing red-brick building could house up to one hundred patients. Peacefully nestled in the woods, the building was the ideal place for the sick to rest and recover.

As medical technology progressed, the need for facilities to isolate tuberculous patients became unnecessary. The sanitorium closed in 1966. It's been more than half a century since the last patient was discharged, but locals still call the building and its grounds Sanatorium Hill. The much-talked-about building now houses the Dane County Department of Human Services—and, if you believe the rumors, a number of restless spirits.

The haunting of Sanatorium Hill is a hotly contested subject among paranormal enthusiasts. There are some who firmly state the building and its grounds are free of all ghosts. But there are others who have gone to the property in search of a supernatural adventure and gotten more than they bargained for while roaming in the nature preserve on the grounds.

Those seeking spirits on the hill with the spooky reputation have found all the evidence of haunting they need in the woods and the small graveyard on the west side of the property. There are countless claims of encountering unexplained cold spots on the land. Ghost seekers have reportedly photographed misty masses, visible only on film, while on the property. They believe these hazy images reveal the spirits who roam the land. There are some who even claim they have been physically touched by an unseen entity while on the property!

Nearby neighbors, and those who have loved ones who died in the building or are interred in the graveyard, dismiss these claims. Naysayers believe the stories are little more than legends perpetuated by young people whose off-trail ghost seeking has damaged the habitat of the nature preserve.

And so, the debate rages on. Is Sanatorium Hill haunted? It depends on who you ask. The legend that surrounds the hilltop property is strong. For nearly a century, tales have been told of strange happenings around that

The former Lake View Tuberculosis Sanatorium. *By Corey Coyle, CC BY 3.0, via Wikimedia Commons.*

building that has been the site of so much sickness and death. Is it just a legend, or are the accounts of paranormal experiences on the land accurate? It seems as if there is only one sure way to find out—to explore the hill for yourself. If you do, be sure to stay on the trails, and be prepared for anything. There is just no telling what you might encounter on your search.

THE MAN IN THE WINDOW

The Stoner House: 321 South Hamilton Street, Madison

It is officially named the Joseph J. Stoner House, but Stoner is hardly the man most associated with the historic building. The Italianate-style home, built of local sandstone in 1855, was donated to the Wisconsin Architects Foundation in 1983. The Wisconsin chapter of the American Institute of Architects (AIA) now uses the building as its headquarters and a museum. While it is registered as both a national and local historical landmark, it might be best known for being the former home of Varley Bond, the man whose spirit is thought to haunt the house.

Bond family matriarch Ellen was a lifelong Madisonian. She met Canadian Varley Bond in 1907, when he moved to town to manage the local Woolworth's store. The couple married in 1910. Both were active members of the community, and they would go on to have four children, all of whom survived to adulthood. Varley became a successful member of the retailer Manchester's executive team, and Ellen received local accolades for the work she did restoring their historic home. The family spent many happy years in their house on Lake Monona's shores.

Tragedy touched the family in 1947, when their oldest son, Walter, was killed in Paris. Walter, a married man with a child, became involved in a wartime romance while serving as a lieutenant in the U.S. Army during World War II. The love affair continued beyond Walter's tour of service. He returned to Paris in the spring of 1947 to reconnect with his paramour, only to discover he had a rival for her affections. Her two admirers fought, and Walter was shot to death.

The prominent Bond family announced the death was an accident, but the truth would soon be known. Before his untimely death, Walter made his French lover, and not his wife, the primary beneficiary of his life insurance policy. This resulted in legal disputes, and soon news spread of Walter's adultery and subsequent murder. The family may have felt the singe of the

The Joseph J. Stoner house. *James Steakley, licensed under CC BY-SA 3.0.*

scandal, but even more than that, Ellen and Varley felt the deep sorrow that comes from the loss of a child. The Bonds were heartbroken, and that sorrow stayed with them for the rest of their lives.

Varley died of a heart attack inside the Stoner house in 1950, when he was seventy-five years old. It is often said that he never recovered from the pain of losing his son and that Walter's death caused Varley Bond's decline. There are those who believe his heart attack was really the effect of his heartbreak. It is reported that he would spend long hours grieving for his firstborn as he stared out at the lake. Ellen remained in the house for a few years after her husband's death and then sold the house in 1957. After the Bond family left, the Stoner house would never again serve as a family home.

Once businesses moved into the building, the reports that something otherworldly was in the home began. People began to see an apparition in the historic home. Described as a figure clad in dark clothes and swathed in a black shawl, the being was also noted to have wispy white hair. The spirit had a long, stern face and, most notably, only one arm. It took very little research for those who saw the entity to discover that Varley Bond had only had one arm. With that evidence, it was concluded that Mr. Bond was the source of the supernatural activity in the Stoner house.

Lorraine Wilke and Rita Wlodarczyk, the owners of Newport Galleries Interior Design, operated their business inside the Stoner House in the years after the Bond family moved out. They had a number of paranormal experiences in their studio during their time in the building. While Rita noted that she sensed a presence in the building, Lorraine had an unforgettable encounter with an entity she believed was Mr. Bond himself. She had an appointment with a client that started strangely. The customer brought her cat to the meeting. Normally docile, the cat resisted going to the second floor of the building, much to the amazement of its owner. After managing to get the cat up the stairs, the pair started their work. Soon, Lorraine excused herself to get something from her office. As she stepped through the doorway of her office, she saw the shadowy figure of a man sitting at her desk. Stunned, she fled the room. The cat must have sensed something was amiss, because when she returned to the meeting, the cat was standing on the floor with its back arched and its fur standing on end. Later, after recovering from the shock of seeing the apparition, Lorraine felt compelled to draw the figure she saw at the desk. When she completed the drawing, she could see that it bore a strong resemblance to the specter that had been spotted in the house over the years. It was all there: the cloak, the wispy hair and the single arm.

Rita was far from skeptical about Lorraine's experience. She had been approached by customers who asked about the firm's new employee. It seemed that a forlorn elderly man appeared in the upper windows of the home late in the night on multiple occasions. Rita assured them that the man looking pensively out onto the water was not with the firm. It seemed as if Varley Bond was at it again.

Things have changed in the home a great deal over the years, but the stories of a supernatural presence in the house remain constant. It has been reported that the AIA keeps a record of the otherworldly happenings that occur in the historic building. It might be worth a visit to check the log of eerie occurrences in the home. Or you could just walk down Hamilton Street some night and check out the windows on the upper floors; you just might catch a glimpse of Varley for yourself.

ON WITH THE SHOW: MADISON'S MOST HAUNTED THEATERS

It seems that just about every old theater in the country is reportedly haunted, and Madison's theaters are no exception. Whether it is the spirit of old performers who remain long after their final curtain call or devoted employees who continue to show up to work despite being buried in their graves, theaters seem to attract and retain restless spirits. Entities in search of an encore can be found at these most famously haunted theaters in Madison.

The Majestic Theater: 115 King Street

The Majestic Theater is an integral part of the downtown landscape. As one of Madison's oldest theaters, the 1906 building has hosted everything from vaudeville shows and silent films to racy rated-X flicks and live music performances in just about every genre.

The ghostly legends that swirl around the historic theater are focused on the building's balcony. There are countless tales of employees seeing a lone man in the balcony long after the theater closed for the evening. A few employees recall the man waving to them from the balcony. Each time the man is spotted, the same events occur. The employee, concerned that a patron is still in the theater, scales the steps to the balcony to walk the man out of the theater. However, when the employee gets to the balcony, there is no trace of the man. Because there is just one way in and out of the balcony, the man's disappearance is always a disturbing mystery. Once the shaken employee realizes the man has vanished into the darkness, fear often replaces curiosity. Few who have encountered the man ever consent to work alone in the theater again.

The haunted Majestic Theater. *James Steakley, CC BY-SA 3.0, via Wikimedia Commons.*

In addition to ghostly man in the balcony, some have reported the eerie feeling of being watched by a pair of unseen eyes while working alone in the building. The spirit may scare employees, but it seems this otherworldly presence may have a soft spot for artists. Performers have described hearing a disembodied voice wishing them good luck for their upcoming show.

Some claim the spirit who lingers in the Majestic is that of a performer who hanged himself in the theater's green room. This legend cannot be verified, as there are no newspaper accounts of a suicide in the building. At this time, the identity of the Majestic Theater specter remains a macabre mystery.

Barrymore Theatre: 2090 Atwood Avenue

Originally known as the Eastwood Theatre, the Barrymore Theatre opened its doors in 1929. The theater has been enchanting visitors ever since with unique features, like "twinkling star lights" in the theater's ceiling that still sparkle to this day. Like most theaters of its era, it hosted films, vaudeville shows and live performances. But, unlike other theaters, this one starred in its own film. The Barrymore Theatre was one of the featured theaters in the 2017 documentary *Haunted State: Theatre of Shadows*. The film captures a paranormal investigation into the reportedly haunted building and tells the stories of those who have had supernatural experiences in the theater.

The film's investigators did not have to wait long for the spirits in the Barrymore Theatre to interact with them. Shortly after they began the investigation, a house light in the theater turned itself on. Within minutes, a heavy metal fire door slammed itself shut. From there, evidence of the haunting continued to mount.

Highlights of the on-camera paranormal investigation of the theater include the appearance of orbs and an electronic voice phenomenon (EVP) voice captured by a spirit box placed on the balcony of the theater. Electronic voice phenomena are recorded sounds that are thought to be the voices of spirits attempting to communicate with the living. These voices cannot be heard without the aid of electronic equipment. In the film, it appears the spirit that inhabits the building has a sexually suggestive exchange with some of the female investigators on the team.

Not all of the paranormal encounters at the Barrymore occur in the theater house. Many who have been in the basement of the theater have claimed to see the apparition of a man. He is dressed in an usher's uniform that

Madison's magnificent Barrymore Theater. *John Margolies, Public Domain, via Wikimedia Commons.*

dates back to sometime in the distant past. When seen, the ghostly theater employee has his arm resting on the banister of the basement staircase.

The documentary film investigators took their flashlights into the basement of the theater and sat in the dark, hoping to connect with the apparition of the former employee. They left a Maglite flashlight on a table in the center of their group and began asking questions of the unseen entity. Maglite flashlights are favored for otherworldly communications because they appear to be easy for spirits to power on and off. Remarkably, the camera crew captured the flashlight powering on and off several times without human intervention in response to questions.

The otherworldly entities that have made the Barrymore their home in the afterlife did not make their final curtain call in the film. If you believe the stories, the spirits linger in the building, waiting to be discovered again and again.

Capitol Theater: 201 State Street

Now part of the Overture Center, the original Capitol Theater was a silent-movie house. It has undergone tremendous modifications since it first opened its doors in 1928. While the structure of the building has changed, one of the things that has remained through the years are the spirits that are said to haunt the old theater after the house lights come on and the curtain closes. In fact, the Capitol Theater is thought to be so haunted that the team at the Overture Center hosts paranormal-themed shows to allow people to experience the ghost for themselves.

Ghost groupies are invited in to hear tales of the apparitions that are rumored to roam the premises. Other paranormal phenomena like cold spots and the unexplained detection of energy have also been reported in

Left: What remains of the Capitol Theater's once-grand entryway. *BrianStanding, CC BY-SA 3.0.*

Right: The landmark Orpheum Theater opened in 1927. *Anna Lardinois.*

the Capitol Theater. Sometimes, lucky ticketholders have the opportunity to hunt for otherworldly entities in areas of the theater that are usually off-limits to guests.

Orpheum Theater: 216 State Street

Some say the Orpheum Theater is one of Madison's most haunted buildings. The Art Deco movie palace was completed in 1927 and provided the capital city with a taste of Hollywood glamour. Generations of Madisonians have filled the theater's seat to see films, live performances and other special events. But there are some who come to the theater just to have a supernatural encounter with one of the building's legendary ghosts.

One of the spooky tales related to this building is that of an usher who reportedly died after falling from the theater's upper balcony. The young male usher, whose life ended beneath the lobby's glittering chandelier, is still seen inside the Orpheum. He has been witnessed seated in the theater house, always alone. Once he is spotted, he is known to disappear without a trace.

Another often-mentioned spirit in the theater is the specter known as Projectionist Pete. Rumor has it this restless spirit was a former projectionist who allegedly committed suicide in the theater. The ghost is said to be a mischievous one and often moves objects in the projectionist's booth. While most people who encounter him think the spirit is benign, there are a few who have had disturbing encounters with Pete. It is reported that the ghost destroyed a stack of plates in a fit of pique after being asked to stop moving objects. Due to the physical capabilities of this entity, the living use caution when interacting with Projectionist Pete.

A night manager from long ago who is still reporting for shifts from beyond the grave is another entity that is believed to inhabit the theater. The hardworking apparition's disembodied footsteps can be heard throughout the building. As he makes his rounds at closing time, the keys jingling from his otherworldly key ring echo in the Orpheum's empty halls. He is sometimes joined by a shadowy figure who has been spotted cleaning the theater.

Not surprisingly, when the theater is closed, the paranormal activity inside the Orpheum is easier to detect. Muffled conversations can be heard in the empty theater. Some have even spotted the apparition of a woman dressed in a lovely gown from a bygone era near the bar. When they move closer to the figure to get a better look at the woman, they find that she has vanished without a trace.

While the dead continue to make an impact on the Orpheum, the living have brought a great deal of their own drama to the historic theater. In 2004, the Orpheum had three fires in the building, and two of the blazes were ruled to be caused by arson. In 2012, the feud between the co-owners of the theater grew so intense that it not only made headlines but also threatened to close the theater. Battles over debts, licensing and shady deals led to a wild tale that rivaled any of the films played on the theater's screen. Fortunately, those tumultuous times seem to be over.

Today, the theater is back to doing what it does best: providing entertainment of all stripes for Madisonans—and providing a home for some of the city's best-known specters!

CHAPTER 5
THE STRANGE AND SPOOKY

W hat is it that makes Madison so strange? Years ago, there was an unsuccessful campaign to make the city motto "seventy-seven square miles surrounded by reality." The phase is often used to acknowledge the city's liberal politics, but could there be something more? Is there something that can't be seen that allows the improbable and outlandish to occur? Following are just a few of the notoriously strange happenings that have occurred in the Greater Madison area.

MYSTIFIED IN MOUNT HOREB

The medical doctors were certain he was faking it. Churchgoers speculated that he might be possessed. The spiritualists believed him to be a prodigy. This is the story of Henry James Brophy, who came to be known as the "Mount Horeb child of mystery."

Henry James "Jimmy" Brophy began living with his grandparents when he was just two years old. During the nine years he lived in the home of his grandfather, Knut Lund, little of note happened in the boy's life. That all changed in 1909, when the eleven-year-old boy and his family began to experience some very strange things in their Mount Horeb household.

It all began on March 9, when Jimmy was entering the side door of the home, which opened into the kitchen. As he walked through the doorway, the child was hit in the back with a snowball that traveled with such force, it knocked the boy off his feet. The slushy sphere smashed onto the kitchen floor, scattering bits of snow and ice all over the room. The boy picked himself up and scanned the yard, looking for the culprit. No one was there. The street was empty. Not a soul could be spotted running from the Lunds' yard. Whoever threw the snowball disappeared without a trace.

The very next day, the unknown snowball tosser struck again. This time, Jimmy's grandparents helped him look for the attacker, but again, there was no evidence that anyone was in the vicinity of the home. Frustrated, the family gave up the search and dismissed the incident as youthful hijinks. The matter was mostly forgotten, until the family sat down for dinner on the night of Thursday, March 11.

Family mealtime began as it typically did, but before the table was cleared, the family experienced such strange events that their lives going forward were forever changed. While Jimmy and his grandparents were seated around the table, the objects in the room began to move, seemingly on their own. Cups flew through the air and crashed to the ground. Bars of soap sailed through the air; hurled by an unseen hand. The spool of thread on the grandmother's sewing machine rapidly unspooled itself. The family was left in awe. They had no idea how, or why, these things happened, but they were frightened. It seemed as if whatever force was responsible for tossing those snowballs at Henry James Brophy may have entered the house.

On Friday, March 12, the situation grew worse. Jimmy's mother was in town for a family funeral and was spending the night in the home Jimmy shared with her parents. She had heard of the shocking events from the night before, but she wasn't convinced. That evening, the family retired to the sitting room, and the visiting mother sat at the organ to entertain her family. Once she began playing, it seemed as if the room came to life. Silverware flew through the air. Furniture moved without human intervention. The stunned family noticed that the aged patriarch was in distress. The unexplained happenings were too much for him, and he grew ill. The family a feared that the man might suffer a heart attack, or worse. In a panic, they tried to soothe him.

The family called for help from the local holy man, the Reverend Mostrom. Mostrom rushed to the home, accompanied by respected community member Sam Thompson. The pair were certain the problem would be easy to solve—and definitely not of supernatural origin. Their confidence waned when they entered the home and a Bible tumbled itself off a table and fell at Mostrom's feet. The grandfather pointed at the Bible, offering it as evidence that something sinister was in the home.

Mostrom took a seat at the organ and played a hymn in an attempt to calm the family. The music only served to rouse the unseen force at work in the room. Young Jimmy quickly called out a warning as a carving knife flew through the air. The point of the knife embedded itself in the floorboard in front of Thompson's feet. The blade, firmly stuck in the floor, wobbled, in front of the man as each person in the room stared in shocked silence.

The action of the night was not quite done. Later, Thompson would have to dodge a hatpin that, like the knife, seemed bound to pierce him. Mostrom and Thompson left that evening, unsure of what they had just witnessed. Both men spent a sleepless night going over the events that occurred in the Lund home and trying to come up with a rational explanation for what they just experienced. If it wasn't supernatural, what was it?

From that night on, things in the Lund home would only get worse. The chimneys of kerosene lamps shattered, despite no one being near them. An unseen hand removed screws in the hinges of the doors, causing them to fall from their doorframes. Family members who thought they were safely tucked into their beds at night were unexpectedly pelted with coal. As the problem worsened, the family struggled to find answers for what was happening in the home.

At the center of each of these events was eleven-year-old Henry James Brophy. The pale child with hazel eyes and curly brown hair would not have been anyone's idea of a rabblerouser. Often described as delicate and sickly, the child had been run over by a carriage and seriously injured when he came to live with his grandparents as a toddler. He recovered and grew into a boy who was described as "normally mischievous" by those who knew him. Some started to suspect that the child was somehow behind these strange happenings; others thought it was unlikely that a boy who was only considered a "fair student" could be the mastermind of an elaborate hoax that fooled so many adults. Still, there was no denying that the otherworldly events never occurred unless the boy was awake and in the home.

People began to offer the Lunds explanations for what was happening in their house. The family rejected the suggestion that objects were moving in the house because the building was "electrified." According to this theory, since the home had both electric power and telephone service, it had an energy field that was causing the mayhem. The grandparents dismissed that theory in favor of the idea that the boy had somehow been secretly hypnotized and remained in a dangerous trance. It was suggested more than once that something paranormal was afoot in the home, an idea that terrified the faithful family.

With no explanations and few options, the family decided to send the boy to live with his uncles in nearby Springfield. If the problems in the home persisted after Jimmy was sent away, the family might consider an exorcism or turning off the power to the home. Before they did anything, they needed to see if the theory was correct, if Jimmy Brophy was responsible for the disturbances in the home. It did not take them long to discover their answer.

As soon as the boy entered his uncle Andrew's home, a pailful of water started spinning on the floor. As the water was being mopped up, Jimmy noticed the mirror hanging on a nearby wall. He turned to his uncle and warned him to remove the mirror from the wall. Andrew laughed at the suggestion, noting that neither of them was anywhere near the mirror. Before the sound of his laughter faded, the mirror crashed to the floor, shattering. In under an hour, it seemed clear that the source of the disturbances in the Mount Horeb home was related to the eleven-year-old boy.

With a better understanding of what was happening, the family turned to folklore to find relief. They were told salt would repel a ghost, so they put a small pouch of salt in the pocket of the boy's trousers. The solution was unsuccessful. Days later, the salt packet would seemingly levitate out of Jimmy's pocket and strike his playmate in the face.

This did nothing to make the boy more popular among his peers. The children of Springfield did not enjoy playing with Jimmy. One youngster fled from a game of marbles with Jimmy because not only did the marbles keep disappearing, but he was also unable to control the marbles when it was his turn to play. Try as he might, he could not get the marbles to move in the direction he was shooting them. Scared and confused, the youngster raced back to his home. After hearing about the odd marble game, Jimmy's uncle Andrew devised an experiment. Andrew reported that he held a cigar box of marbles in front of the boy, and the glass orbs jumped out of the box on their own, without the boy having any contact with the box.

When his stay in Springfield was over, the uncles returned Jimmy to his grandparents' home in Mount Horeb. Andrew brought along a basket of eggs to give to the Lunds. He placed the basket of eggs on the table, then watched in amazement as an egg launched out of the basket and hit the boy in the face. As Jimmy wiped the yolk from his face, it seemed to all who had seen the egg fly toward the boy on its own that it was time to get some outside help for this perplexing problem.

A number of medical doctors met with Jimmy and could find nothing physically wrong with him. These experts were dismissive of the reports of airborne household items and were convinced that the boy was a faker who was at the source of the so-called disturbances. Finding no relief from the medical community, the faithful in Mount Horeb turned to God for a solution. The churchgoers held a prayer meeting in the Lund home, which only resulted in increased activity inside the house.

It was when the family met Dr. George Kingsley that they finally got some answers, albeit not the ones they may have hoped to find. Kingsley, a doctor and a spiritualist, proclaimed the boy was a gifted medium. He believed the chaotic events in the home were the result of the youngster being unable to control his great powers. The spiritualist was certain that with time and training, the boy would learn to harness his psychic skills, and the havoc in the house would cease.

After hearing of the boy's powers, clairvoyants came to see Jimmy. They proclaimed that three spirits surrounded him, two women and one man. When his mother heard this, she wondered if one of the spirits was a former babysitter who had cared for Jimmy when he was an infant. The woman was a known spiritualist. She considered the possibility that when the woman died, she may have transferred her powers to the child.

Not only did the clairvoyants see spirits, but they also offered explanations for why these strange occurrences only happened in the home and only when few people were present. It was noted that Jimmy attended school without incident, and when large groups of people showed up in the home to witness the phenomena, they left disappointed. One time, two hundred people packed themselves into the Lund home, gaping at the shattered glass and broken china strewn throughout. They came to see objects fly through the air, but the wreckage of past occurrences was all that was available to them that night. The spiritualists sensed that crowds quashed the spirits, which was probably a relief to the boy, who would grow agitated and sometimes cry when crowds descended on the home.

All these events had a negative impact on the elderly Lunds. Things got so difficult for the family that they posted an official announcement in the *Mount Horeb Times* newspaper, begging the townspeople for understanding and urging them to stop spreading gossip about the events in the home. This plea may have made some in the Mount Horeb community blush with guilt, but it did not stop the story of Henry James Brophy from becoming national news.

A definitive explanation for what happened in Mount Horeb in 1909 has never been given. Henry James Brophy disappeared from the pages of history after the strange happenings of that year. Those who lived through the events remain divided about what truly occurred. There are some who are certain the clever boy was the source of the mysterious phenomena. Others suspect the events were genuine supernatural occurrences. Was a poltergeist attached to the lonely boy who rarely saw his mother? Could the child have been a medium, as the spiritualists believed? To this day, there are no answers to these compelling questions, but as long as the story remains in the imaginations of Wisconsinites, those familiar with the Mount Horeb case will never tire of asking them.

Infamous Shoes

She was the Madison girl who made national news in the fall of 1900. Considered pretty and refined, the young woman was the apple of her parents' eyes. A good student and an active member of the Presbyterian church, Miss Myrtle E. Downing was a well-respected member of the Madison community. That is, until she got a new pair of shoes.

Light tan in color, the dainty shoes were made of "pliable and durable" leather. Myrtle had them custom-made for her by a local shoemaker. She was exceptionally proud of the shoes and wore them often. What was so unusual about these shoes that they would garner national attention? The shoes were made of human flesh.

Despite the girl's reputation for refinement, Myrtle had exceptionally peculiar tastes, particularly for a woman living in turn-of-the-century Madison. She had an appetite for the macabre. Myrtle displayed a human ear on the wall of her bedroom. A human skull grinned down at the girl from a bedside bookshelf. While her peers were horrified by the relics, Myrtle delighted in her grisly treasures.

Myrtle had a friend who was attending medical school in Chicago. The body of an unidentified man who had been shot to death was delivered to the school for students' use. As Myrtle's friend gazed upon the corpse in front of him, he thought of the girl and developed a plan.

Knowing Myrtle's penchant for the ghoulish, the student decided to give her a truly one-of-a-kind gift. The student skinned the leg of the corpse, then tanned the flesh he removed from the leg to create a swath of leather. The young man carefully packed up and sent the treated human flesh to Myrtle, anticipating that she would be delighted with the gruesome gift. She was.

Myrtle took her unholy treasure to the shoemaker, telling them the origin of the leather only after the shoes were complete. After taking the shoes from their horrified maker, she slipped them onto her feet, thrilled with the gruesome slippers. The exacting craftsman was economical in their use of the material, so Downing had enough of the human leather remaining to commission a pocketbook. She reveled in the shiver that ran down the spines of those she told of her plans for a handbag made of human flesh.

The girl wore her new footwear all over town. She'd coax compliments from her friends about the dainty slippers. Once the shoes had been sufficiently admired, Myrtle would gleefully reveal that they were made from the remains of a skinned man. She found untold satisfaction in the horrified looks of revulsion on the faces of those who had unknowingly praised the shoes just moments earlier. Myrtle, and her awful shoes, soon became the talk of Madison.

The story was too shocking to stay in Madison, and it soon spread to Milwaukee. From there, the story was picked up by the national media. Reports of Myrtle's human flesh footwear appeared in newspapers from coast to coast in November 1900.

After an infamous autumn in which the strange girl with the ghastly shoes was thrust into the national spotlight, she slipped back into obscurity. But the tale of Madison's most morbid shoes lives on.

SOMETHING STRANGE ON OLD GHOST ROAD

Seminole Highway

Today, we call the road Seminole Highway, but years ago, when it wound around Daniel Damon Bryant's farm, it was known as Bryant Road. In the time before streetlights and sidewalks, when people traveled the rural road at night, they carried a lantern or walked by the light of the moon. It was in that era that the stretch of road earned the name it has yet to shake: Ghost Road.

Ghost Road was aptly named; it was haunted by a ghost that scores of late-night travelers encountered on the road. The specter would appear as a softly glowing white mist. Sometimes, the entity would emerge from the brush that lined both sides of the road. Its movements were not predictable. It appeared from both sides of the road, so many a traveler would walk down the middle of the road in an attempt to steer clear of the ghostly form.

It is said that after the spirit appeared, its shimmering form would follow the nighttime traveler. The ghost would always disappear just as suddenly as it arrived. The entity never spoke to or attempted to harm the frightened walkers, yet the spirit was dreaded and feared by all who traveled the lonely road after dark.

Not to be outdone by the terrified walkers who encountered the otherworldly spirit on the road, nearby farmers claimed to experience a ghostly pony on Bryant Road. They reported that the pounding hoof beats of an unshod pony could be heard at night trotting up and down the road. Yet, in the daylight, there was no trace that the animal had been there.

Despite the numerous claims of paranormal experiences on the road, it was never determined who the restless spirit was that roamed Bryant Road, or why the spirit continued to linger among the living. It was the habit of people in the area to gather around campfires late at night to tell the story of Ghost Road. Sometimes, they would speculate that the spirit was a young Native boy. Other said it was spirit of a murdered man who was buried in a nearby cemetery. The stories thrilled and terrified generations of Madisonians but never led to any answers. The mysterious spirit gave no clues to its identity.

Just who, or what, haunted Bryant Road remains unknown. They say that as the area became more populated, sightings of the shimmering spirit became scarce. Automobiles replaced horse-drawn buggies, and sometime in the late 1930s, old Bryant Road was renamed Seminole Highway. It is thought all the changes to the area chased the spirit away. Yet there are some who believe the spirit remains on the land.

Is Ghost Road nothing more than a legend, or does the spirit remain, harder to spot with all the lights and traffic but still there, as it has been since Madison's early days?

SPIRITUALIST SUICIDES

During the winter of 1927, there was a rash of suicides of young college men across the nation. Many wondered if these deaths were provoked by the inclusion of psychology courses in college curriculums. On January 23, 1927, a twenty-year-old University of Wisconsin premed student, Walter Cassels Noe, died by suicide. The death shocked the city, but no one in Madison blamed psychology courses for his death. The truth behind the suicide was far stranger than anyone could have imagined.

Noe was found in his bedroom with a gunshot wound to his forehead by his mother when she returned from Sunday morning services at Grace

"Spirit" photograph, supposedly taken during a séance, 1901. *Library of Congress, LC-DIG-ppmsca-40857.*

Episcopal Church. The student left behind two letters; one was addressed to a girl whose name was never published and the other to his parents. To his family, he wrote of spiritualism and explained that he wanted to discover "what lies beyond." He outlined his plan to explore the afterlife and stay connected with the living after his death. Included in the note was a directive for his father to tell Bob that he would come back in spirit form and visit him at "midnight on Monday and again on Friday."

Bob was Robert Horton, a fellow member of the Delta Kappa Epsilon fraternity. The next Monday, Bob and the other fraternity brothers, who were mourning the loss of the well-liked Noe, dutifully waited in silence as the midnight bells chimed. But there was no sign that their friend was present. No voice from beyond called to them. There was not even a rustle of fabric or an errant breeze in the room signaling the presence of a spirit. They repeated the ritual on Friday, as the letter instructed, but the results were no different. Despite his plans while on earth, Noe did not reach out from beyond the grave.

Within days, the story grew stranger. It was discovered that Noe had visited a friend, Joseph Moore, while the students were on winter break just weeks earlier. Shockingly, Moore died by suicide shortly after Noe's visit. His body was discovered by his parents on December 31, 1926. In the note he left behind, he said he had already experienced "all that life has to offer." Like Noe's letter, Moore's included allusions to spiritualism and communicating with the living after death. After Moore's family learned of Noe's death, they came to believe that the friends had made a suicide pact.

It wasn't just the Moore family who thought the young men planned their deaths together. Noe's physics class lab partner gave a number of interviews in the days following his death. He claimed Noe became obsessed with suicide after classes resumed on January 4 and talked of nothing else. He even stated that Noe asked whether he thought a gunshot blast to the head or the heart would have a greater likelihood of being fatal. While reporting on the supposed pact, the newspapers also continued to note the psychology studies Noe was exposed to on campus as another possible reason for his death. Many people were wary of the relatively new field of study and attributed scores of societal ills to the study of psychology.

Noe was laid to rest in Forest Hill Cemetery on January 26, with his fraternity brothers acting as pallbearers for the young man's casket. Noe's body was gone, but with headlines like "Student Kills Self to Probe the Hereafter," and "Fear Others Involved in Noe Suicide Pact," this story wasn't going anywhere.

The men of Delta Kappa Epsilon pose with their house mascot in 1923. *University of Wisconsin Collection.*

Clerics of all denominations shared their thoughts on Noe's death with both their congregations and the press. No member of the religious community made a bolder claim than Cora Pullon, the pastor at the First Spiritual Church of Madison. In an interview with the *Capital Times*, the pastor stated that a midnight, the spirit of Noe appeared to her in the Woman's Building on Gilman Street. She saw the vision of a "hazy spiritualistic form hovering over the heads of two university students." She recognized one of them as Noe. She heard Noe say, in what she described as a "very faint and hardly discernable" voice, "I am very sorry and though I know now what I thought to be true, I have my actions to atone for." She stated that the young men were accompanied by an "old guiding spirit." Additionally, Pullon revealed that Noe did visit the fraternity house as his letter promised, but the students were unable to sense his presence.

All this proved to be too much for at least one member of the fraternity. By April 1927, a sophomore in the house reportedly had a nervous breakdown and was committed to a sanitarium in Wauwatosa. The young man, said to be "in serious condition," thought of little other than the suicide after the untimely death of his friend Noe.

Today, all traces of the fraternity house that once stood on Pinckney Street have vanished. One can only hope the mystics of the day were wrong and Noe is not caught somewhere between the here and the hereafter, desperately trying to communicate with the living, who are unable to hear him.

Mary Hayes Chynoweth: The Spiritualist Healer

Born Mary Folsom in New York in 1825, the woman who would become one of the country's most celebrated psychic healers moved to Waterloo, Wisconsin, in 1849 to become a teacher. She spent fewer than four decades of her life in Wisconsin, but during that time, she made a lasting impact as one of the best-known spiritualists in the state.

The future leader lived a conventional life until the spring of 1853, when she was a twenty-seven-year-old schoolteacher. She would later tell her biographer of an event that happened while she was doing chores in the family kitchen. She recalled, "Suddenly, some unknown Force pressed me down upon my knees, helpless....Of my own will I could not move nor see nor speak; but a compelling Power moved my tongue to prayer in language or languages unknown to me or to my father." Her father, a Baptist minister, witnessed these events. Chynoweth claimed "the Force" told her she would spend the remainder of her life healing others.

Soon after the Force revealed itself to Chynoweth, she married Anson Hayes, a Waterloo farmer who was also the cousin of President Rutherford B. Hayes. He never doubted her abilities and was reluctant to start a family with the spiritualist, thinking it would prevent her from carrying out her life's work. However, Chynoweth believed the spirits came to her to let her know she would have three children. True to this prediction, the couple did have three children, and two of them lived into adulthood. When their third child, Charles, was born blond and blue-eyed—unlike the rest of the family, who had dark hair and dark eyes—Chynoweth took it as a sign from the spirits that he would not live into adulthood. Unfortunately, she was correct. The child died at age three.

It was during this time Chynoweth began to rise in prominence as a practitioner of spiritual medicine.

She took no credit for her miraculous healing powers. Instead, she saw herself as a conduit for the "universal power of love and light." With the abilities bestowed on her by God, she could do amazing things. She claimed she had the power to "see" into bodies, as if they were transparent, in order to diagnosis diseases. It is said she could heal the sick by placing her hand on them and transferring their illness into her own body. Witnesses claimed to see the blisters, tumors and other ailments disappear from the afflicted and form on Chynoweth's own body after she laid her healing hand on the patient. She was also given the ability to communicate with the sick in their native tongue. Despite only knowing English, she was able to spontaneously speak in German, Polish, Danish and other languages when working with her non-English-speaking patients.

Beyond the spiritual abilities granted to her, the healer was also deft at preparing herbal remedies. She believed in the power of optimism to help patients heal and was an advocate of a vegetarian diet. She abstained from all alcohol, tobacco and coffee.

Chynoweth had the trust of some pretty well-connected Wisconsinites. Among those who came to her for healing were Senator William Vilas and Wisconsin Supreme Court justice William Lyon.

It was the spiritualist leader's ability to foresee the future that made her a wealthy woman and helped her found the town of Hurley, Wisconsin. "The Power" had helped the spiritualist financially in the past. Perhaps this was because she did not charge for her healing services. She received visions of economic downturns and had premonitions of when to buy and sell assets.

In the spring of 1883, Chynoweth told her now-adult sons about a business prospect presented to her by "the Power." The men, both University of Wisconsin–educated lawyers, were practicing in the Ashland area when their mother was struck with a vision. The spirits told her to go into mining and led her to the spot on the map that would be profitable for the family.

The men were doubtful as they looked at the area Chynoweth pointed to on the map: a densely forested, unoccupied place about forty miles from Ashland. They protested, claiming they knew nothing of mining, but the spiritualist said she had been assured that they would get all the assistance they needed.

Help soon arrived in the form of a geologist who had explored the Gogebic Iron Range, a range of hills that spans northern Michigan and Wisconsin that is rich in iron ore deposits. Guided by "the Power," Chynoweth told the men exactly where to dig. On their first attempt, they discovered some of the richest iron ore deposits in the entire range.

Chynoweth also advised a few of her friends from the spiritualist community to invest in mining. Among those who followed her guidance was Morris Pratt. He would use this windfall to open the Morris Pratt Institute, a college for spiritualism, in Whitewater. The school is largely responsible for the town's moniker: the "Second Salem."

Before long, the family had opened the Germania and Ashland mine. These lucrative mines needed employees and a place to house them, and soon, the town of Hurley was founded. Chynoweth was disappointed to see the booming alcohol and vice trade in the town that was established to run her mines. As a remedy, she opened and funded a school to educate the children of the town. Six of them would go on to attend college at the spiritualist's expense.

Chynoweth continued working as a healer while the family fortune grew. Now wealthy, the sixty-three-year-old saw forty-one-year-old patient Thomas Chynoweth for an eye ailment. She offered the Madison-based lawyer an herbal remedy, and his eye quickly cleared. The pair continued to see each other long after Chynoweth recovered. A whirlwind romance bloomed, much to the dismay of the woman's two sons. The couple eventually wed, but their bliss was short-lived; Chynoweth died after only ten months of marriage.

Now a two-time widow, the aged psychic healer moved with her sons and their families to San Jose, California, in 1887. She would go on to found the True Life Church in 1903, acting as both pastor and editor of its widely read newsletter. In 1905, her life ended peacefully at age eighty inside her California mansion. Her last words were, "I have never wronged anyone."

MARY HAYES CHYNOWETH'S RELATIONSHIP with Morris Pratt still impacts Whitewater to this day.

Pratt purchased land in Whitewater, Wisconsin, and built a college devoted to spiritual study. Originally called the Temple of Science, the school opened in 1889. Not everyone in the town of just 4,300 people was happy to see the school open. Dubbed "Spooks Temple" by townspeople, the school did little to court the affections of the populace. At the school's opening ceremonies, the keynote speaker, noted medium Mrs. Luther from Indiana, detailed the ways in which mainstream religions were inferior to spiritualism. The town was insulted by the message, and soon the evils of spiritualism were being preached from every pulpit in the town. Eventually, Pratt took to publishing challenges in the local paper and inviting local religious leaders to come to the school and debate spiritualism. It was a misguided effort to teach the town about his beliefs.

Before long, the school changed its name to the Morris Pratt Institute and began offering general education classes in addition to its curriculum on spiritualism. In 1947, the institute moved to Milwaukee, and the building was purchased by the nearby college. The facility, which had been used to teach students the art of séance and other spiritual practices, was used as student housing for teachers in training. An old building with a mysterious past plus young people away from home for the first time was the perfect recipe to launch hundreds of eerie tales about mysterious happenings in Whitewater.

To this day, rumors swirl around Whitewater's reportedly occultist past. There are those who believe that a coven of witches has been practicing the black arts in the town since its inception. The legend states the witches use the town's underground tunnels for nefarious deeds and designed the town using demonic geography, known as the Witch's Triangle, to curse the land and all its residents. To plot the infamous Witch Triangle, note the locations of the town's three cemeteries on a map; they form an isosceles triangle. It is believed that anything inside the Witch's Triangle is in danger of being cursed.

A Place Where the Earthly Veil Is Thin

Wonewoc Spiritualist Camp: 304 Hill Street, Wonewoc

Locals call it Spook Hill. Some call it a "religious summer camp." It is one of the twelve remaining spiritualist camps in the United States. Wonewoc Spiritualist Camp sits high atop a wooded bluff overlooking the small town of Wonewoc, about seventy miles northwest of Madison. People have been gathering on the land to connect with the other side ever since a group of spiritualists arrived on the property from New York in 1874. Since then, the faithful have gathered among the trees to commune with the spirits of those who have left the mortal coil.

Believers from all over flock to the camp to connect with the dead. At the camp's peak, as many as 1,500 people arrived each summer day seeking guidance and education. The number of visitors is smaller now, but little else has changed over the last one hundred years. The camp offers workshops on topics like past life regression, automatic writing, spirit drawing, aura reading and scores more otherworldly topics. Visitors can attend medium-led spiritual services and participate in spirit circles, the camp's preferred name for what is often called a séance. Perhaps the biggest draw are the mediums, who can be booked for thirty- or sixty-minute readings.

It should go without saying that visitors to the camp must be comfortable mingling with ghosts. According to the mediums, spirits are everywhere on the grounds. Not everyone can see them, but there is no doubt they are there. A central idea in the spiritualist faith is that life is endless. The spirits of those considered to be the dead can and do communicate with the living through a medium. Those who practice the faith often describe spiritualism as the study of science, philosophy and religion as a single subject, rather than three distinctly separate subjects.

There is no charge to visit the camp. Guests are welcome to explore the woods or visit the celebrated Healing Tree. The tree is said to have miraculous healing powers, backed by the countless testimonials from visitors who have been cured of scores of ailments.

The intrepid might choose to spend the night on the grounds in one of the guest cabins that were built in the 1920s. While the cabins are reasonably priced, one might generously classify the accommodations as "rustic." The cabins do not have bathrooms and show the effects of time, weather and the occasional vandal. One of the best-known cabins on the grounds is the ominously numbered Cabin 13. At its door is a lightbulb they say has been continuously burning, day and night, for more than thirty years. The inexplicable bulb has been dubbed the "spirit light."

The camp shows few signs of the modern era, but they are there. While the dining room no longer serves meals, snacks and souvenirs can be purchased in the camp office. Modern travelers might want to visit the camp website to book time with the mediums of their choice before they make the pilgrimage to the rural retreat. If you visit, Wonewoc Spiritualist Camp asks of you only one thing: that you keep an open mind.

CHAPTER 6
MADISON'S MYSTERIOUS WATERWAYS

Just what is it that people claim to see in Madison lakes? Is it a log? An uncommonly large fish? Maybe some kind of yet-to-be-identified sea serpent? Or is it what some claim it must be: Winnebozho? Part of Ojibwe culture, Winnebozho is thought to be the creator of plant and animal life.

Sometimes it is described as having a long, spiked tail; other times, its large jaws and blazing eyes have been noted. Each new sighting brings new details about the monster's appearance. Blamed for overturning canoes with its tail, chasing sailboats and even uprooting piers, the creature once was a fearsome presence in Madison's waterways.

Whatever the monster is, it has made appearances in all the lakes in Madison's chain of lakes, and the stories of these strange sighting are still told to this day.

LAKE MENDOTA

Perhaps the first documented sighting was in the 1860s, when a couple took their canoe out to Governor's Island. One of their paddles struck what they initially thought was a log, and they were startled when what they believed was a piece of wood dove under the water. The frightened pair quickly paddled on, but the event stayed with them. They shared their strange encounter only after others began to suggest that an unknown entity lurked beneath the waters of Madison's largest lake.

A scenic postcard of Lake Mendota. *J.A. Fagan Publishing, Madison, Wisconsin, public domain, via Wikimedia Commons.*

Vintage scene of Lake Mendota. *Detroit Publishing Company photograph collection, Library of Congress, LC-D4-4647 [P&P].*

Later, fisherman Billy Dunn captivated crowds in the summer of 1883 when he claimed to have had an encounter with the beast. According to the *Wisconsin State Journal*, he and his wife were fishing at eleven in the morning when Dunn spotted a black object "moving threateningly" toward his boat. He saw the outline of a snake in the water as the object grew nearer. Dunn was shocked when he saw a "reptile head" emerge from the water, rising at least two feet above the waves. He could then see that the beast had light skin mottled with white spots that the man described as "slimy."

As it approached the boat, it revealed its long, forked tongue, black as coal. The beast flickered its inky tongue at the man and showed its fangs. In an act of self-defense, Dunn hit the beast on the back of its neck, momentarily stunning the creature. Quickly recovering from the blow, the animal sank its teeth into the oar, forcing Dunn to repeatedly strike the beast until it released the oar and disappeared beneath the water. Once safely onshore, Dunn proudly displayed the oar, with black fangs still embedded in the wood. This souvenir from the battle in Lake Mendota was later sold to a Chicago musician.

In his collection of sea serpent tales, Wisconsin historian Charles Brown recounts that in 1917, a University of Wisconsin–Madison student recovered what looked like an exceptionally large, tough fish scale from the shore at Picnic Point. He took the scale to his professor, and legend has it the man identified it as a scale from a sea serpent. Shortly after this strange identification took place, a man finishing on Picnic Point reported a terrifying encounter with a mysterious being that rose from the lake. The creature had a snake-like head, "large jaws," and "blazing eyes." Frozen with fear, the man watched the animal slither in the water until he could take no more. Returning to his senses, the man ran from the water's edge, abandoning his fishing rod and gear.

That same year, a pair of sunbathing college coeds had a surprising encounter with the beast. While the couple basked in the sun, the young woman felt a tickle on the soles of her feet. Thinking her date was attempting to get fresh with her, she rolled over to scold him, only to discover it was not her beau tickling her. She came face to face with a hideous creature she would later describe as having the head of a snake or a dragon. The curious sensation she felt on her feet? That was the creature's forked black tongue flickering across her soles. With her toes still intact, the couple fled to the safety of a nearby fraternity house.

LAKE MONONA

In 1892, an unidentified resident of nearby Oregon told his local newspaper of his terrifying encounter with the mysterious beast. According to a news report, the man rented a boat and rowed it out to what he thought would be an ideal fishing spot.

As he prepared his fishing rod, a monster rose from the murky depths of Monona. The man claimed that as soon as it appeared, the creature began to attack him. The beast, which he described as at least twenty feet long with a flat head, dove under the rowboat in what the man believed to be an effort to overturn the boat.

The frightened fisherman dropped his fishing pole into the lake, grabbed both oars and rowed furiously to shore. He managed to avoid contact with the creature but swore to the reporter from the *Oregonian* that he would never enter Lake Monona again, not "for all of the money in capital city."

That same summer, two teenaged boys encountered the creature as they paddled between Hoboken Beach and Winnequah. From about seventy-five feet away, they spotted the fast-moving beast. They reported that its head was similar to that of a dogfish (also known as a bowfin), but it did not slither through the water like as snake, as others described. Instead, this creature propelled itself through the water in an up-and-down motion, similar to that of a dolphin.

People frolicking at the nearby beach spotted the beast as well. Panicked swimmers cleared the waters upon its approach. Those near land claimed the creature was somewhere between ten to fifteen feet long, with an estimated

"Downtown Madison, Wisconsin, the Capitol, & Lake Monona from Olin Park," by jimflix! *Licensed under CC-BY-NC-ND 2.0.*

"Bigmouth Bowfin," by Phil's 1stPix. *Licensed under CC BY-ND 2.0.*

circumference of around one foot. It quickly swam away, leaving everyone who saw it shaken but unharmed.

Perhaps the most famous encounter with the creature on Lake Monona happened in 1897. It was a warm June day when Eugene Heath spotted the much-talked-about creature from shore. Determined to rid the city of this scourge, Heath aimed his gun at the mysterious beast and fired two shots. Rather than flee the attack, the beast turned around and swam toward the gunfire. Soon after the animal changed course, the men watching the scene from the shore lost sight of the creature in the waves.

Most townspeople believed that Heath's bullets did not hit the creature, or if they did, they did not injure the mysterious animal. Later that same night, eyewitnesses from around Lake Monona claimed the creature was spotted gliding along the moonlit lake.

Lake Waubesa

A lone fisherman on Lake Waubesa claimed to have had a shocking encounter with a lake creature, shortly after scales from a sea serpent were reportedly found on Picnic Point. While anchored in the lake, the man cast his line and then noticed the water around him churning. He was stunned as a great beast rose to the surface of the water. The man described the creature as between sixty and seventy feet long and dark green in color. The animal appeared to be sunning itself on the surface of the water. Without disturbing the creature, the startled man quietly released his anchor and rowed to shore. When this vacationing Illinoisian fisherman first told his tale, people doubted both his eyesight and his sobriety. But an encounter later that summer changed a few minds. A couple was swimming near Waubesa Beach when they encountered something strange in the water. The pair claimed to have seen an unfamiliar creature rising from the water. As its glittering eyes stared at the swimmers, they fled from the water in terror. Could this be the same beast that made itself known in the other lakes?

LAKES KEGONSA AND WINGRA

These smaller lakes were not immune to sightings of a mysterious creature. Eyewitnesses claimed to have spotted a beast on Lake Kegonsa that they identified as a dragon. This dragon was seen near Collady and Williams Points.

Lake Wingra also had a sighting of a water monster, but the results were even less dramatic than the sightings on Kegonsa. Charles Edward Brown's seminal 1942 book *Sea Serpents: Wisconsin Occurrences of These Weird Water*

Tranquil Lake Wingra. *Yinan Chen, public domain, via Wikimedia Commons.*

COLLADAY POINT, LAKE KEGONSA.

"Stoughton WI 1907 Lake Kegonsa before Development Colladay Point EC Kropp Card 2916 Postmarked," by UpNorth Memories—Don Harrison. *Licensed under CC BY-NC-ND 2.0.*

Monsters in the Four Lakes, Rock, Red Cedar, Koshkonong, Geneva, Elkhart, Michigan, and Other Lakes states that upon further investigation, the Lake Wingra monster turned out to be a very large snapping turtle that was ensnared in fishing equipment.

The sightings of the mysterious beast have slowed considerably since the late 1800s, but that does not necessarily mean the lakes are no longer the home of an unknown creature. Those who find themselves on the chain of lakes or sailing down the Yahara River should stay alert for signs of the unnamed beast swimming nearby. Strange things are known to lurk beneath the surface of these waters.

CHAPTER 7
THE EERIE OUTSKIRTS

Madison may have more than its fair share of ghosts, but that does not mean the surrounding areas do not have their own haunts, legends and specters. No matter which road you take out of town, it is likely you are heading into a stretch of land with its own spine-tingling tales of the supernatural. Some of Wisconsin's most haunted locations are rumored to be a short drive from the city. Consider any of these spook-tacular locations for your next day trip.

TERROR AND TALES FROM TALIESIN

Taliesin: 5481 County Road C, Spring Green

One of Wisconsin's most popular tourist attractions is also the location of one of its most horrific crimes.

Visitors from all over the world come to Spring Green to see Frank Lloyd Wright's sprawling eight-hundred-acre estate, Taliesin. The visionary architect built the home as a tribute to his married lover, Martha "Memah" Bouton Borthwick Cheney. Their scandalous relationship burned with passion at the onset and ended with the blow of an axe and an arson's match.

Their tale of forbidden love begins in 1903, when Edwin Cheney hired Wright to design an Oak Park, Illinois home for his family, Wright, at the time a married father of six, worked closely with Cheney's wife as he

Left: The famous architect Frank Lloyd Wright (1867–1959). *Public domain.*

Right: Mary "Mamah" Bouton Borthwick Cheney (1869–1914). *Public domain.*

created plans for the Cheney home. The pair quickly fell in love and began an affair so fervent they decided to leave their spouses. Catherine Wright refused to grant her husband a divorce, but the couple was undaunted. Soon, Frank and Memah abandoned their families and ran off to Europe in 1909 to continue their relationship without interference from their spouses. When the pair returned to the United States, they found themselves in need of a home. Branded as adulterers, they were shunned in Chicago, so they went to Spring Green, where Wright's mother owned property, and he began building Taliesin in 1911. He meant the home to be a tribute to his love for Memah.

In the summer of 1914, Memah's children, who lived with their father in Chicago, came to Spring Green for a visit during their school holiday while Wright was away on business. On August 15, 1914, Memah and her two children, eight-year-old Martha and twelve-year-old John, were seated for lunch on the porch of the prairie home. In the nearby dining room, Wright's employees were also gathered for lunch. Tending to both groups that day was thirty-year-old "jack of all trades" Julian Carlton and his wife, Gertrude, who was busily cooking lunch in the kitchen.

Carlton served soup to Memah and her children and then stepped away from the table. Moments later, he returned to the table, approaching the seated woman from behind. Without a word of warning, he raised an axe in the air and delivered a blow to the back of Memah's head so powerful that it split her skull wide open. Her son, John, was next to die. Carlton swung the axe at the boy, and he suffered from a fatal strike to his forehead. Young Martha rose from the table and fled the scene of carnage, but her small eight-year-old legs did not carry her far. Carlton easily caught up with the girl and repeatedly struck her in the head with his now-bloodstained axe, killing her. Within minutes, Carlton had massacred the trio.

Meanwhile, Wright's employees were eating lunch, oblivious to the slaughter occurring just yards from where they dined. As the men ate their soup, they heard what a survivor, as quoted in *Storied and Scandalous Wisconsin*, remembered as a "sloshing sound" that he would later liken to "water hitting the outside of the door." Within moments, the dining room was engulfed in flames. The men didn't know it then, but after Carlton killed Memah and her children, he doused the dining room, the porch and even the freshly murdered bodies of the dead in gasoline and then tossed a lit match onto the deadly trail.

Taliesin after it was ravaged by the fire set by Julian Carlton. *Public domain.*

When the men tried to flee the dining room, they discovered they were locked inside the room. When they managed to break open the lock, they found the door was barricaded shut. Trapped, the desperate men barreled through the barricade, only to discover an axe-wielding Carlton waiting outside the room. Terror overcame the men as they believed death, either by flame or axe blade, was imminent.

Summoning all of his courage, a nineteen-year-old draftsman, his clothing and hair ablaze, managed to jump out of the dining window and avoid Carlton's swinging axe. He and two other men, who were both burned and wounded by axe blows, escaped the property and ran one-half mile to Taliesin's nearest neighbor to get help. When assistance finally arrived, Wright's famous building was consumed by flames, and six lay dead. Days later, one of the men who initially escaped the attack succumbed to his injuries, causing the death toll of this horrific day to climb to seven.

What motivated this brutal attack remains a mystery. After the massacre, Carlton evaded capture on the secluded property for hours. After an exhaustive search, he was eventually found hiding in the unlit furnace of the home. In an effort to escape justice, he attempted suicide by swallowing hydrochloric acid.

Carlton was arrested and received medical attention for his self-inflicted wounds while he was in jail. His burns were extensive and seemingly untreatable. Carlton died soon after from starvation, as he was unable to eat or drink due to the damage caused by the ingestion of the acid. To this day, there is no explanation for what happened that bloody summer day.

Wright was devastated by this massacre, which spared his life but destroyed his home, studio and happiness. He built Taliesin for Memah, and he was determined to rebuild the home to keep her light shining in this world. With a few modifications, Wright kept the plans for the new home nearly identical to Memah's home. The reconstructed home, Taliesin II, was completed in 1915, and Wright moved in with the woman who would become his second wife, Miriam Noel. In 1922, Catherine finally agreed to a divorce, and the architect wed Miriam in 1923.

Despite the rebuilt home and his new marriage, Wright remained deeply unhappy. Tragedy would revisit him at Taliesin on a lonely night in 1925. While Wright was sitting in the dining room that was a replica of the one in which the massacre had occurred, he noticed smoke billowing into the room. When he rose to follow the smoke, he discovered his bedroom was ablaze.

Once again, flames consumed the room he shared with his lover. Wright fled the fire, and while no one was injured in the blaze, high winds fed the flames, and the home was destroyed for a second time. Later, it was determined that lightning had struck a telephone line, transferring the surge to his bedside phone, which started the blaze. There are some who think it is more than bad luck that plagued Wright. Was this lightning strike to the architect's bedside telephone a message from beyond the veil, as some believe? Whatever the true cause of the fire, Wright was determined to remain on the land, so he rebuilt Taliesin a third time.

Since the site has borne witness to so much tragedy, it is unsurprising that restless spirits still roam the grounds. Visitors in tune with the supernatural have reported smelling gasoline and smoke while near the main house. The most popular and often-repeated story is that the spirit of Memah still roams the grounds. A cottage on the grounds, known as Tan y Deri, is where the bodies of Memah and her slaughtered children were taken shortly after the massacre. Today, the cottage is rumored to be the site of a great deal of paranormal activity. It is said Memah's energy fills the building, causing doors and windows to fly open seemingly on their own. Lights often turn on by an unseen hand, and people claim to hear the disembodied voices of ghostly children. A number of people have claimed to see Memah herself, clad in a white gown, peacefully roaming the grounds.

If Memah's spirit still waits to be reunited with Frank, her efforts are in vain. Sadly, these star-crossed lovers remain apart. Memah Borthwick's final resting place can be found at the nearby Unity Chapel Cemetery. Frank Lloyd Wright intended to be buried at Unity Chapel Cemetery as well, in his family plot and near the woman who inspired what some say was his greatest work. When the architect died in 1959 at the age of ninety-one, he was interred in the Unity Chapel Cemetery. While his grave markers, inspired by his work on the Guggenheim Museum and the Coonley Playhouse, are still on the property, the remains of the famous man are not.

When Wright's third wife, Olgivanna, died in 1959, she left instructions to have Wright's body exhumed and cremated. She further ordered that his ashes be mixed with her own and scattered over Taliesin West, in Arizona. These actions were controversial and done without the consent of the children from Wright's first marriage. Those who knew Olgivanna thought her decision reflected her fondness for the Arizona property, but others believe this was a spiteful act, motivated by jealousy over the love Wright felt for the woman who was the first to call Taliesin her home. Whatever the third Mrs. Wright's reasons, she succeeded in separating the lovers one final time.

THE PHANTOM HITCHHIKER

Who is he? Where does he come from? What is his connection to Wisconsin's Highway 12? The fact that there are no answers to these questions only seems to make the strange tale of the Highway 12 hitchhiker all the more fascinating—and spooky.

Designated in 1917, Highway 12 is an east-to-west roadway that runs diagonally across nearly 340 miles of the Badger State. From the Wisconsin and Illinois border and northwest to Minneapolis, the highway moves through both farmland and cities. It became part of the Interstate Highway System after 1926 and now stretches from Washington State to Detroit, Michigan. Parts of the midwestern portion of this road, including the Wisconsin leg, are named in honor of the Iron Brigade, the only "all-Western" group of fighting men to serve in the Civil War. Led by Brigadier General Rufus King, the group was made up of volunteer infantry regiments from Wisconsin, Indiana, Illinois and Michigan.

So, how did a small stretch of historic Highway 12, which runs between Baraboo and Wisconsin Dells, become so infamous? The road seems to have an otherworldly hitchhiker. For years, people have reported seeing a bedraggled man walking along Highway 12. Described as a lean man with a dark beard and long, greasy black hair, he is always clad in a tattered green army jacket. He can be spotted both day and night, eager to catch a ride from cars traveling in the area near Ski Hi Road. As the hitchhiker walks along the shoulder of the road, cars speed past him. But he doesn't stay in their rearview mirrors for very long.

Motorists who drive past the hitchhiker are always surprised when, miles up the road from where they first spotted the man, he appears again, just ahead of them on the side of the road. Stunned drivers puzzle over how the hitchhiker could have bypassed them while they traveled at a rate of at least fifty-five miles per hour down the two-lane road. Was it possible for this solitary walker to have traveled faster than a car? Could someone else, driving much more quickly down the highway, have picked him up, only to drop him off a mile or two down the road? Drivers who pass him a second time are always shaken by his unexplained presence.

Over the years, a few brave souls have claimed that they stopped for the phantom hitchhiker. Apparently, the Highway 12 hitchhiker is no Resurrection Mary; he always disappears before he reaches the vehicle offering him a ride. For many, his unexplained disappearances are further evidence that the phantom hitchhiker is undeniably a paranormal being.

Who he is and why he is roams this road is anyone's guess. Due to his appearance, some speculate that he may have lived during the 1970s, as his unkempt appearance and jacket seem to fit into the style of the era. There are those who think the mysterious man is tied to the road because he was struck by a drunk driver and died on Highway 12. While both stories are plausible, the truth of who he is and why he is there remains unknown. In a story filled with unknowns, one thing is certain: Highway 12 is a terrible place to pick up a hitchhiker.

THE BRAY ROAD BEAST

Bray Road, Elkhorn

On a lonely stretch of rural road in Elkhorn, Wisconsin, prowls a mysterious creature that has sent shivers of fear through all those who have seen it. No two eyewitness descriptions of this creature match, but all who have seen it agree that the being is terrifying and it is neither a man nor any known animal. Dozens who claim to have encountered the creature believe it is a werewolf. They call this frightful being the Beast of Bray Road.

While people have reported seeing this creature for decades, it wasn't until beloved chronicler of Wisconsin oddities Linda Godfrey investigated the sightings that the Beast became widely known. Godfrey covered the sightings while working for the Elkhorn-area local newspaper, the *Week*. She investigated a rash of reports of the creature in the late 1980s and early 1990s. The creature was reported prowling around Bray Road, which is a single-lane rural road surrounded by farmland. Soon, the creature became associated with this dark stretch of sparsely populated road. Before long, the mysterious creature was given the name Beast of Bray Road. Far from solving the mystery, the release of Godfrey's articles detailing the sightings of the creature only brought more reported sightings. The Beast garnered national media attention but no additional answers about what was terrorizing this lonely stretch of road.

While descriptions of the Beast vary in specifics, it is often described as a creature that stands on two legs and is anywhere between five and seven feet tall. It is reported as having a shaggy coat of long, dark hair, and some witnesses have stated that the fur is streaked silver or gray. While most have described the creature as having a head similar to that of a German shepherd, with an elongated muzzle and pointed ears, a few claim that the

Beast has a head that more closely resembles an ape than a dog. Although witnesses are not consistent about all aspects of the creature's appearance, there is one trait all who have encountered the Beast of Bray Road agree on: the intense, penetrating stare from the animal's cold, yellow eyes shook them to their souls.

Godfrey's reports uncovered that those who saw the animal were struck by its human characteristics and panther-like run as it fled from the unexpected encounters with people. Some presented evidence of what appeared to be deep claw marks on the cars whose drivers encountered the Beast. Godfrey spoke to a few witnesses who were so unnerved by their experience with the Beast that they were convinced the creature had some occult connections.

The first known sighting of the Beast was in 1936 by a nighttime security guard at St. Coletta's, a home for the developmentally disabled. The rural, isolated campus is best known for its most famous resident, Rosemary Kennedy, who, as the result of a failed lobotomy, was confined to the institution from 1941 until her death in 2005. While patrolling the grounds after midnight, the security guard encountered a creature clawing the ground. As the man approached, the animal advanced toward him, rising from its haunches to reveal an erect height of more than six feet. The stunned man said that the animal was covered in dark hair and smelled strongly of putrid

St. Coletta School as it was when the Beast made an appearance on the grounds. *Author's collection.*

flesh. The creature stared into the man's eyes, holding his gaze steadily as it sounded a deep, unearthly growl. The terrified guard quietly crept away, feeling the heat of the beast's eyes boring into his back while he prayed the animal would leave him unharmed. Unscathed yet shaken, the frightened man never again encountered the beast, but many others have.

Despite the best efforts of those who wish to discount the sightings, no credible evidence has ever proven that the creature seen by witnesses was a wolf, bear, stray dog or any other known animal. Does a werewolf live in Walworth County? As unbelievable as it sounds, those who have encountered the mysterious beast think this might be a real possibility. The creature has been written about countless times and was even the subject of a 2005 film, aptly titled *The Beast of Bray Road*. Both the skeptical and the true believers can be seen by the carful, driving down Bray Road with their headlights blazing, in hopes of solving this mystery by identifying the beast.

For now, the identity of the Beast of Bray Road remains a mystery.

THE BADGER STATE'S STRANGEST SPECTER

The Ridgeway Ghost: Route 151 in Iowa County

Iowa County's Ridgeway Ghost may be Wisconsin's most famous—and certainly busiest—ghost. Found on the twenty-five mile stretch between Dodgeville and Blue Mounds along what is now Route 151, this restless spirit has been scaring travelers since 1840. The strange apparition has taken on many forms, sometimes appearing as a pig, a dog or a sheep. When it appears in human form, it has shown itself as a man with a whip, an old woman and even a headless horseman, but some of the best-known stories about this mysterious specter describe it as little more than a dark form.

This ghost of many shapes is also credited with many different methods of causing mayhem on the often-traveled road. Often, the spirit will appear quite suddenly along the roadside. It has been blamed for removing the wheels on traveling wagons, intentionally scaring horses to cause wrecks and sometimes even leaping onto moving wagons and throwing the driver off. After these encounters, driverless wagons would often return home, pulled by exhausted horses that had been running for hours. On farms along the road, the ghost has been seen pumping water at a well and has been blamed for milking cows dry as they stood in their fields.

"Ridgeway WI," by railsr4me. *Licensed under CC BY-NC-ND 2.0.*

The road was a dangerous one, and not just because of the eerie happenings along the remote route. This stretch of road connected the mining towns and was dotted with inns and saloons. The road was often traveled by hard-drinking gamblers who moved down the line hustling miners out of their paychecks and the prostitutes who often joined them on the journey. Many travelers would rather have encountered the Ridgeway Ghost than the rough group of outlaws who used the road under the cover of darkness.

The Ridgeway Ghost made national news when the *New York Times* published an article in 1902 featuring three deaths rumored to be caused by the phantom. The piece briefly mentions an anonymous dressmaker who encountered the specter on the dark roadside and chased it, only later to die of shock and fright. More details are given about the three encounters that Dr. Cutler, a Dodgeville physician, had with phantom. Cutler first met the Ridgeway Ghost as he returned home after attending to a patient. As he drove his carriage along the dark lane, a shadowy figure suddenly appeared on the pole that connected his horses to the wagon. The terrified horses reacted to the ghostly presence by running wild, while Cutler, unable to control the animals, held onto the reins for dear life. He escaped shaken but unscathed—and unbelieved. Dr. Cutler was known to be a tippler, and those who heard the harrowing tale assumed his experience was a drunken misadventure rather than a supernatural encounter.

Cutler insisted that he was sober when he encountered the Ridgeway Ghost, but his story was largely disbelieved until he met the ghost a second time. The lane was dark and deserted as he passed the same location where he had spotted the ghost the previous year. As he reached the bend in the road, the phantom appeared next to him on the seat of the carriage. It rode with him for several heart-stopping miles before disappearing as quickly as it had appeared. After Dr. Cutler's second encounter with the Ridgeway Ghost, people were more apt to believe him. Sadly, he was not able to enjoy his reformed reputation for long. The doctor crossed paths with the specter a third time, and the experienced taxed him so greatly that he later died of fright.

John Lewis soon joined the doctor and the dressmaker on the list of those who died after encountering the Ridgeway Ghost. Lewis was a Cornish farmer who had a reputation as a hale and sober man. He was the father of Evan Lewis, a professional wrestler who is credited with introducing the sleeper hold to the sport. Ridgeway townspeople state that John taught Evan the wrestling skills that led him to national fame. Late one evening, John was returning to his farm after helping a neighbor butcher livestock. He decided to take a shortcut home that required him to scale a small stone fence and cross a field. As he left the road, he met the Ridgeway Ghost, who appeared in the form of a menacing man. The tall, dark figure loomed over Lewis, who decided to walk past the figure while tightly clutching the butcher knife he had used just minutes before.

As Lewis stepped past the figure, it moved to block his path. The farmer lunged toward the phantom with his butcher knife. As the cleaver sliced through the empty air, Lewis found himself "hurled into the air as if in the vortex of a cyclone, pounded, crushed into insensibility," according to the *New York Times*. His broken body lay in the field until he was discovered the next day and carried home. Before he succumbed to his injuries just a few hours later, he made the dying declaration that his life was taken "by supernatural agency."

The identity of this spirit remains as mysterious as its actions. Some believe the Ridgeway ghost is the spirit of a peddler who was murdered in Sampson's Saloon in the 1840s. The man stopped for the night seeking a bed and water for his horse and was never seen again. Others claim the ghost was created during the same era on a bleak night at the notorious McKillip's Saloon. It is said that two brothers, aged fourteen and fifteen, entered the saloon and encountered a drunken mob who tormented the boys. As the violence escalated, one vicious patron grabbed the fifteen-year-old brother and tossed him into the roaring fireplace, burning the boy alive.

To the sounds of his brother's tortured screams, the younger boy fled, but he was later discovered frozen to death in a nearby field. In both cases, it is thought the Ridgeway Ghost was created when an innocent person met a grim end on the well-traveled road.

Today, the Ridgeway Ghost has been elevated from a collection of frightening tales to the mascot of the Village of Ridgeway. The dangerous being has been reimagined as a friendly specter who can be seen smiling from the village's water tower. Reports of encounters with the Ridgeway Ghost began to taper off as automobiles became the primary mode of transportation along the road, but most believe the phantom still lingers along this road, as it has for centuries.

DEAD MAN (STILL) WALKING

The Walker House: 1 Water Street, Mineral Point

Nestled into the hills of the Driftless Area lies Wisconsin's third-oldest town, Mineral Point. Settled in 1827, it was named for the rich deposits of lead and zinc in the area. The booming mining business attracted Cornish miners to the area, and their cultural impact is still evident in the charming town—and, if you believe the legends, one very tenacious ghost.

Over the years, many have said the historic Walker House is haunted. The structure, parts of which date back to 1836, is said to be near the execution spot of condemned murderer William Caffee. It is believed that the spirit of the man still lingers where he spent the final moments of his life.

On February 23, 1842, William Caffee attending a housewarming party. Men far outnumbered women in the frontier mining town, so people used dance cards to ensure all the guests at the party had the opportunity to take a twirl around the floor. Tempers flared when Caffee declared his name had been skipped in the rotations of dancers. The altercation moved outside, and soon Samuel Southwick of Gratiot Grove was dead from a single bullet to the chest, fired by Caffee.

Justice moved swiftly in the Wisconsin Territory, and soon the case was before Judge Mortimer Melville Jackson, who ruled that "blood must be paid with blood" and ordered Caffee be hanged for the first-degree murder of Southwick.

Caffee was a memorable condemned man. He traveled to the location of his execution sitting atop his coffin, while he used two empty beer bottles to

"Mineral Point 48," by carnwrite. *Licensed under CC BY-NC-ND 2.0.*

pound out a funeral march. Before being led to the gallows, he requested "a raw slice from the heart of Judge Jackson" as his final meal. The more than four thousand spectators who gathered to watch the hanging reveled in the show. Caffee's bravado did nothing to save him; before the sun set on November 1, 1842, William Caffee's dead body was swinging from the end of a rope. To this day, no one knows where the body of the executed man was laid to rest.

Despite the current owners' insistence that the landmark inn and restaurant is not haunted, there are countless others, including former owners, who have sworn they have experienced paranormal activity at the Walker House. Strange happenings began to be recorded in 1964, when renovations began on the long-abandoned property. In 1978, David Ruf bought the property and rented a second-floor apartment to a college student. Within days, the tenant reported the doorknob of his bedroom door would turn at night, seemingly without human intervention, and the nocturnal jiggling of the door was accompanied by sounds so strange and otherworldly that it prompted the student to pack his bags and leave.

During this same time, staff begin to report unusual activity in the kitchen. The clanging of pots and pans was heard coming from the empty kitchen, and two former employees are certain they observed a bread box be moved by an unseen hand while in the room. Employees were afraid to be alone in the kitchen, and the fear only increased when a waitress reported a supernatural entity grabbed her ponytail and held her hair high in the air while she was working in the kitchen. She was shaken but unhurt by spine-tingling event.

It appears the paranormal activity is not limited to the kitchen area or to the employees. Female guests have claimed to have felt their hair being stroked by something that could not be seen, and both men and women have sensed a presence behind them, only to turn around and find no one there. Often the feeling that someone is near is accompanied by the sound of heavy breathing. Disembodied footsteps have been reported on all three floors of the building, particularly in the first-floor pub. Those who spend time in the pub report feeling unexplained cold spots throughout the room.

While many have experienced paranormal activity in the building, very few have reporting seeing a ghost on the premises. Despite the rarity of such sightings, those who have seen an apparition are certain the specter is William Caffee. While making an inspection of the second-floor porch, Ruf turned the corner to see a figure in a grey miner's jacket and denim pants. As his eyes rose from the figure's dusty clothing, he saw a black felt hat sitting directly on its shoulders. The entity before him had no head. Shaken, he quickly turned away and locked the door. When he looked back, the figure had vanished.

All these eerie happenings have led the *Food Network* to name the Walker House Wisconsin's most haunted restaurant. Does an unearthly spirit dwell in the landmark? Scores of former employees and guests claim they have had supernatural experiences in the building, while the couple who have owned the Walker House since 2012 state that nothing paranormal dwells beneath its roof. Visiting for yourself is the best way to decide if William Caffee still lingers near the site of his execution.

A Glimpse into the Past

Hauge Log Church: 1359 County Highway Z, Blue Mounds

It is hard to know which is the bigger draw for curious travelers, the history or the lore of this historic white building. The Hauge Log Church (pronounced HOW-ghee) was one of the first Lutheran churches built in western Wisconsin. Erected in 1852 by its congregants, the twenty-by-twenty-foot oak log building is designated as both a local and a national historic landmark. The building was at the center of the Norse community in its early days, used as a house of worship for two different congregations and as a schoolhouse. Abandoned in 1887 in favor of a larger building, Hauge Log Church was restored in 1927 and has been a beloved landmark for generations.

Paranormal enthusiasts are attracted to the lore that swirls around the historic building. Local legend says the church is haunted by a parishioner who died in the building long ago. According to the often-told tale, the building has been struck by lightning twice. These lightning strikes left the building standing but killed a woman who was inside the building. There are many who believe the spirit of this unfortunate woman remains inside the church.

Sensitive visitors have reported seeing an apparition in the building. She is described as a short, plump woman with long, blond hair that is twirled into a bun and secured on the top of her head. Those who have seen her note that it appears she has burns covering one side of her face.

The Hauge Log Church, built in 1852. *Library of Congress, HABS WIS,13-DALY.V 1–2. Public domain.*

The pews of the historic Lutheran church. *Library of Congress, HABS WIS,13-DALY.V 1–4. Public domain.*

It is the disfigurement of her face that has led people to assume they are encountering a long-dead parishioner.

Interestingly, this spirit is heard more often than she is seen. For years, there have been reports of a woman's screams coming from the property as the sun sets. It has been observed that when groups visit the property, some can hear the woman's voice very clearly, while others in the same group can hear nothing at all. A few have even reported hearing the woman while inside the church. They describe the spirit's voice as an angry one, and while her words cannot be understood, the spirit makes it clear that visitors are an unwelcome intrusion.

In the nearby cemetery, several of the church's founding members are buried, including the man who cut the first log during the construction of the church. There are some who say there is more in the graveyard than historic headstones. Believers in the supernatural claim there is a spirit—or possibly even multiple spirits—that still lingers among the graves. The sensitive have reported feeling bursts of icy air brush past them as they strolled through the grounds. More than one person has described an energy in the area that caused the fine hairs on their arms and the backs of their necks to stand at attention. There are those who believe it is the spirit of the woman inside the church that roams the property.

Not only is this woman suspected of making her presence known in the cemetery, but it is also said that she makes use of the rustic swing hanging from a nearby tree. The sturdy swing has been known to rhythmically sway back and forth even on days when the air is still. People have heard the squeak of the heavy rope that suspends the wooden board used as a seat from the stout limb of the tree, but the swing appears to be empty.

Are these tales true? The best way to find out is to see for yourself. The Hauge Log Church is open to the public and worth a visit for both history lovers and those interested in the otherworldly. Before you go, just remember—it might be best to prepare to be scared.

BIBLIOGRAPHY

Bauer, Scott. "Hearing from Dead." *Spokesman-Review* (Spokane, WA), August 25, 2007.

Brown, C.E. (Charles Edward). *Sea Serpents: Wisconsin Occurrences of These Weird Water Monsters in the Four Lakes, Rock, Red Cedar, Koshkonong, Geneva, Elkhart, Michigan, and Other Lakes.* Madison, WI: Wisconsin Folklore Society, 1942.

Brown, Michael. *Haunted State: Theatre of Shadows.* Hungry Lion Productions, 2017.

Busch, Jason. "The 7 Most Haunted Businesses in Madison." *In Business*, October 31, 2019. https://www.ibmadison.com/the-7-most-haunted-businesses-in-madison/.

Capital Times (Madison, WI). "Behind the Stoner House, a Tale." May 26, 2003.

———. "Broods over Death of Cassels Noe." April 18, 1927.

———. "Lemberger Is Held." October 5, 1921.

———. "Madison Spiritualist Claims She Talked with Noe." January 31, 1927.

———. "Says Youth Framed Pact in Holidays." January 25, 1927.

———. "Trial Set for Beating Suspect." May 16, 1979.

Chicago Tribune. "A Death Trap." November 9, 1883.

Clark, Brian E. "Madison's Wonder Bar Steakhouse Has Mob History, Ghosts." *Milwaukee (WI) Journal Sentinel*, October 31, 2014. http://archive.jsonline.com/features/travel/madisons-wonder-bar-steakhouse-has-mob-history-ghosts-b99380667z1-281121762.html.

Curtis, W.A. "Some Wisconsin Ghosts." *New York Times*, December 7, 1902.

Custer, Frank, "Did a Water Beast Live Here?" *Capital Times* (Madison, WI), June 21, 1977.

Doehlert, Betsy. "Do Ghosts Walk Arboretum Glade?" *Capital Times* (Madison, WI), October, 31, 1977.

Elbow, Steven. "Theater of the Absurd." *Capital Times* (Madison, WI). June 27, 2012.

Erickson, Doug. "The Ghost of the Old Baraboo Inn." *Wisconsin State Journal* (Madison, WI), July 5, 2005.

Evening Star (Washington, D.C.). "Boy's Uncanny Antics." May 16, 1909.

Falkenstein, Linda, "They See Dead People." *Isthmus* (Madison, WI), July 13, 2007. https://isthmus.com/news/cover-story/they-see-dead-people/.

Fannon, Emilee. "The Ghost at Great Dane Pub & Brewery." WDJT Milwaukee. October 17, 2021. https://www.cbs58.com/news/the-ghosts-at-great-dane-pub-brewery.

Gerber, Amber. "Waterloo Pioneer Shared 'Gift' with Others." *Courier* (Sun Prairie, WI), October 29, 2008. https://www.hngnews.com/waterloo_marshall/community/article_720bd33c-28ca-554a-8adc-cd895400e6e7.html.

Green Bay Republican (Green Bay, WI). "News Report." February 19, 1842.

Hathaway, Aaron. "Behind the Curtain of Madison's Concert Venues, the Undead Put On Their Own Performances." *Badger Herald* (Madison, WI), October 27, 2015. https://badgerherald.com/features/2015/10/27/behind-the-curtain-of-madisons-concert-venues-the-undead-put-on-their-own-performances/.

Hauge Log Church Preservation Association. "Hauge Log Church." Retrieved May 18, 2021. http://www.haugelogchurch.org/.

Herman, Ellie. "Wisconsin Union Theater: A Ghost Story," *Terrace Views* (blog), October 18, 2017. https://terraceviews.org/wisconsin-union-theater-a-ghost-story/.

Janik, Erika. *Odd Wisconsin*. Madison, WI: Wisconsin Historical Society Press, 2007.

Khoury-Hanold, Layla. "The Most Haunted Restaurant in Every State." Food Network. Retrieved February 16, 2021. https://www.foodnetwork.com/restaurants/photos/haunted-restaurants-america.

Lardinois, Anna. *Milwaukee Ghosts and Legends*. Charleston, SC: The History Press, 2019.

———. *Storied and Scandalous Wisconsin*. Guilford, CT: Globe Pequot Press, 2020.

Lemberger, Mark. *Crime of Magnitude: The Murder of Little Annie*. Madison, WI: Prairie Oak Press, 1993.

Little, Sean, *Family Ghosts*. Sun Prairie, WI: Spilled Inc. Press, 2019.

Maine, D'Arcy. "Seven of the Most Haunted Venues in Sports" ESPN, October 20, 2022. https://www.espn.com/college-football/story/_/id/27962267/in-honor-halloween-seven-most-haunted-venues-sports.

Markowitz, Lisa. "Haunted History: The Legend of Science Hall." Wisconsin Foundation & Alumni Association, October 1, 2019. https://www.uwalumni.com/news/haunted-history-the-legend-of-science-hall/.

Miller, Mike. "UW Coed Testifies about Axe Beating in Library." *Capital Times* (Madison, WI), November 13, 1979.

Muscatine (IA) News Tribune. "Her Slippers a Man's Skin." November 8, 1900.

National Park Service. "Forest Hill Cemetery Soldiers' Lot Madison, Wisconsin." US Department of the Interior. https://www.nps.gov/nr/travel/national_cemeteries/wisconsin/forest_hill_cemetery_soldiers_lot.html.

National Register of Historic Places. Forest Hill Cemetery, Madison, Dane, WI, 74000070.

Norman, Michael. *Haunted Heartland*. Madison: University of Wisconsin Press, 2017.

paranormalgeneration. "PG S02E04—Pub Poltergeist." YouTube, November 27, 2011. https://www.youtube.com/watch?v=TcxBA359JiY.

Patenaude, Joel. "Haunted Hallowed Ground at Forest Hills Cemetery," *Madison Magazine*, August 31, 2021. https://www.channel3000.com/haunted-hallowed-grounds-at-forest-hill-cemetery/.

Peterson, Gary. "Nameless Ghost Stalks Walker House." *Capital Times* (Madison, WI). October 28, 1982.

Peterson, Iver. "Reburial of Frank Lloyd Wright Touches Off Stormy Debate." *New York Times*, April 10, 1985.

Pleasanton (KS) Observer. "A Fateful Fall." November 17, 1883.

Rath, Jay. "Madison Monsters: Meet Our Ghosts, Ghouls, Witches and Werewolves." *Isthmus* (Madison, WI), October 30, 2014. https://isthmus.com/news/cover-story/madison-monsters-meet-our-ghosts-ghouls-witches-and-werewolves/.

Reinherz, Barbara. "Save 'The Gates of Heaven.'" *Wisconsin State Journal* (Madison, WI), November 29, 1970.

Rose, Patricia. "Haunted Houses in Madison, Wisconsin." *USA Today*, February 8, 2021. https://traveltips.usatoday.com/haunted-houses-madison-wisconsin-56504.html.

San Francisco (CA) Examiner. "'True Life' Faith Guides the Politics of Hayes' Brothers." March 30, 1904.

Scott, Beth, and Michael Norman. *Haunted Wisconsin.* Minnetonka, MN: North Wood Press, 1980.

Seely, Ron. "Ghostly Stories of Madison," *Wisconsin State Journal* (Madison, WI), October 31, 1995.

The Stoner House: A Piece of History. AIA Wisconsin, October 13, 2010. Originally published 1984.

Strub, Sherry. *Ghosts of Madison, Wisconsin.* Atglen, PA: Schiffer Publishing, 2008.

Willoughby, Alfred. "U.W. Student Enters Suicide Pact to Prove 'Spirit' Theory." *Capital Times* (Madison WI), January 24, 1927.

Wisconsin Historical Society, Wisconsin Architecture and History Inventory. 123 E Doty Street, Madison, Dane, Wisconsin, 17004.

———. "Drummer Collapses, Dies During Concert at Memorial Hall." March 12, 1950.

———. Frautschi Funeral Home and Apartment Building, Madison, Dane, WI, 115945.

———. Joseph J. Stoner House, Madison, Dane, WI, 102184.

———. "Lembergers Are Subpoenaed to Appear at Coroner's Inquest." September 11, 1911.

———. "Mt. Horeb Mystery Is Scouted." April 2, 1909.

———. "Register of the Charles E. Brown Papers, 1889-1945." http://digital.library.wisc.edu/1711.dl/wiarchives.uw-whs-wis000hb.

Wisconsin State Journal (Madison, WI). "A True Snake Story." June 23, 1883.

ABOUT THE AUTHOR

Anna Lardinois tingles the spines of locals and visitors to Milwaukee through her haunted historical walking tours known as Gothic Milwaukee. She is the author of *Milwaukee Ghosts and Legends*, *Storied and Scandalous Wisconsin*, *Shipwrecks of the Great Lakes* and several Spooky America titles for young readers: *The Ghostly Tales of Milwaukee*, *The Ghostly Tales of Flint*, *The Ghostly Tales of Baraboo* and *The Ghostly Tales of Prescott*. The author, a former English teacher, is an ardent collector of stories, an avid walker and a sweet treats enthusiast. She happily resides in a historic home in Milwaukee that, at this time, does not appear to be haunted.

Visit us at
www.historypress.com
....